à la
di Stasio

* *

* **APPLIED ARTS** AWARD – **PHOTOS** *
* **APPLIED ARTS** AWARD – **GRAPHIC DESIGN** *
* **GOURMAND WORLD COOKBOOK** AWARD – **BEST TELEVISION COOKBOOK, FRENCH** *
* **CUISINE CANADA**, GOLD MEDAL – **BEST FRENCH-LANGUAGE COOKBOOK** *

* *

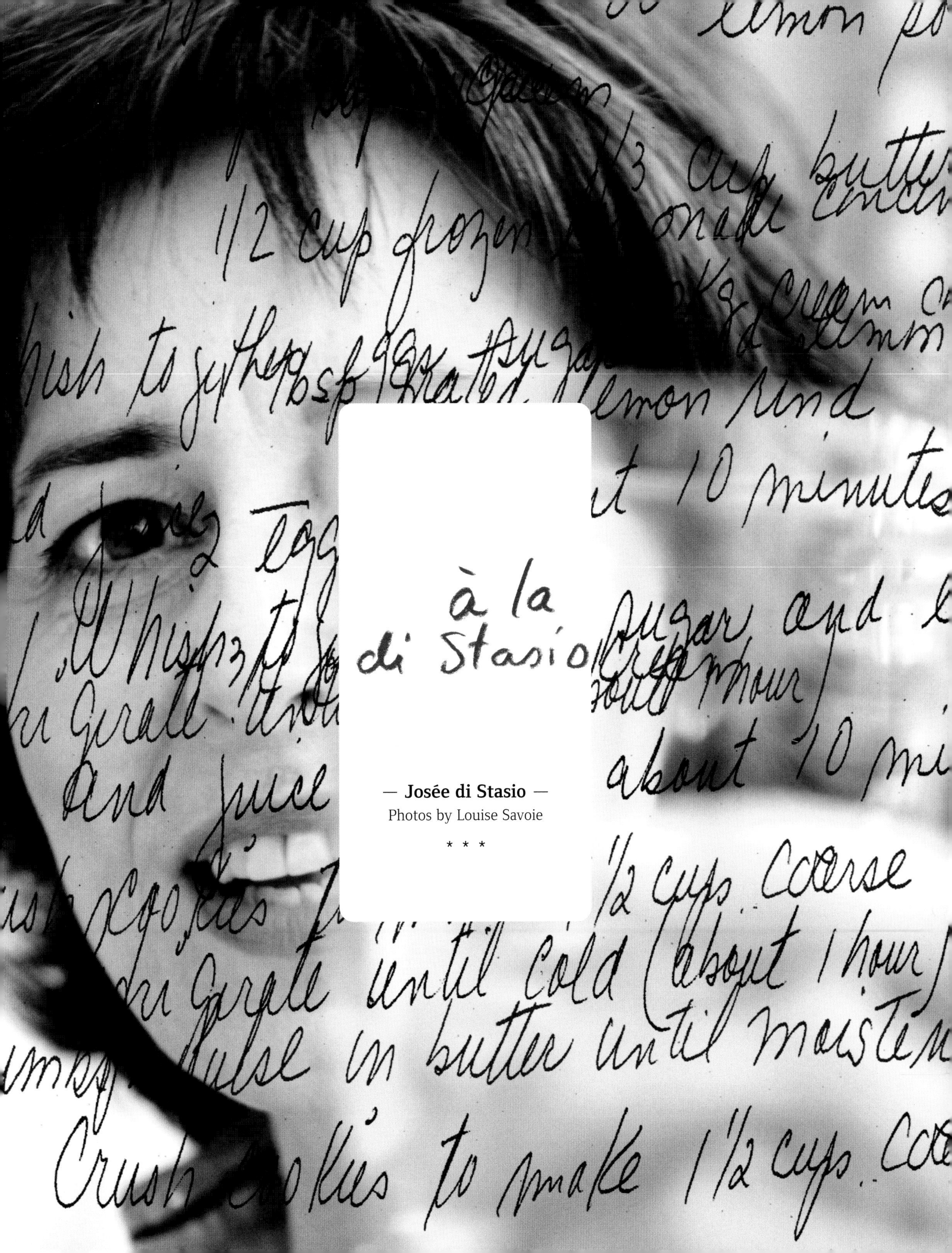

à la di Stasio

— **Josée di Stasio** —

Photos by Louise Savoie

* * *

Transcontinental Books

1100 René-Lévesque Boulevard West, 24th floor

Montreal (Quebec) H3B 4X9

Tel.: 514-340-3587 / Toll-free 1-866-800-2500

www.livres.transcontinental.ca

**Bibliothèque et Archives nationales du Québec and Library
and Archives Canada cataloguing in publication**

Di Stasio, Josée

  À la di Stasio

  Translation of: *À la di Stasio*

  Includes index.

  Text in English only.

  ISBN 978-0-9738355-9-5

  1. Cookery. I. Title.

TX714.D5213 2008   641.5   C2008-941723-2

Production coordinator **Marie-Suzanne Menier**

Translation **Nancy Lynn Bogar**

Proofreading **Tina Anson Mine, Austen Gilliland**

Food stylist and consultant **Stéphan Boucher**

Assistant stylist **Jade Martel**

Assistant photographer and black and white photo printing **Alain Fournier**

Colour photo digitization **Shared Production Centre of Montreal, Transcontinental Media**

Page and cover design **orangetango**

This book was originally published in French under the same title
by Flammarion Québec and Josée di Stasio © 2004

Printed in Canada

© Transcontinental Books and Josée di Stasio, 2008 (English version published in Canada)

Legal deposit — 4th quarter 2008

National Library of Quebec

National Library of Canada

We acknowledge the financial support of the Government of Canada through
the Book Publishing Industry Development Program (BPIDP) and the Government
of Quebec through the SODEC Tax Credit for our publishing activities.

For information on special rates for corporate libraries and wholesale purchases,
please call **1-866-800-2500.**

For my mom,
who gave me
a true love of food

1 cup sug

12 oz bitter

4 eggs

4 egg yol

1 Tbsp van

1 cup flo

at together

— Table of Contents —

* * *

* * *

* * *

As a little girl, I spent hours watching my grandmothers cook.
It was my favourite game, and I still haven't stopped playing.
—
Yes, cooking is an addictive game, one that is gourmet and so very sensual.
What a pleasure it is to stroll through the markets, make discoveries and be inspired!
Cooking spices up my life, warms it, beautifies it.
In my view, the best way to meet people is around a table.
That's where conversations come to life, where we discover and reinvent
the world by savouring all its flavours.
—
This book is a selection of recipes I gleaned through reading,
attending meetings and gatherings, and taking trips, as well as recipes from my family and my gourmet friends.
Some are classics, others contemporary, yet they are all simple.
This is a friendly, warm type of cuisine, seasonal in that it uses the best products
without requiring special techniques or sophisticated utensils.
—
For me, as for many of you, cooking is first and foremost intuitive.
I hope my recipes will serve as a guide. Let your imagination and love of food go free,
and always remember that the main ingredient is enjoyment.
—
Enjoyment is the key word of this book, one I've wanted to write for a long time
and which is my own way of receiving you all at my table.

* * *

— Nibbles —

* * *

No-Cook or Low-Cook Cocktail Hour Platter

At cocktail hour, offer your guests a platter of nibbles without spending hours in the kitchen.

* * *

*I love cocktail hour.
It's the start of that special time
when we can pause and relax.*
—
*One, two or three bites,
even the simplest, are always
well received. I particularly like
this format, which can replace the
appetizer. This way, you can take
all the time you want, and then
sit down for the main meal.
So easy, and so convivial!*

* * *

Some gorgeous **melon** wedges, peeled, seeded and seasoned with lots of pepper. A magnificent, effortless dish. You can also take full advantage of fig season, serving them sliced with prosciutto or other meat.
—
A block of **Parmesan** (or other hard cheese) with a knife to slice off chunks.

A **seasonal vegetable** (radishes, fennel, celery heart with leaves), casually arranged, accompanied by good-quality plain or lemon-flavoured olive oil (p. 176) and seasoned with good-quality sea salt.
—
On **croutons** (p. 172) or seasonal vegetables, serve a commercial spread (there are very good ones available) or your own refrigerated spread, or a selection of garnishes:
_ Sun-dried tomato pesto
_ Smoked Salmon Mousse (p. 18)
_ Chicken Liver Mousse
  with Figs (p. 21)
_ Caponata (p. 98)
_ Black Olive Spread (p. 14)
_ Scrambled eggs with chives
  and fish roe
_ Hummus mixed with sun-dried
  tomato pesto
_ Roasted red and yellow peppers,
  peeled and julienned, with a drizzle
  of oil, garlic, salt and pepper
_ Quartered cherry tomatoes with a
  chiffonade of basil and mint, garlic,
  a drizzle of oil, salt and pepper
_ Drained ricotta mixed with pesto

A bowl of **nuts** roasted for a few minutes on a baking sheet at 350°F (180°C).
—
A dish of good-quality marinated **olives**.
—
Sausages or dried meats (bresaola, dried duck breast or prosciutto) with melon, pear or papaya slices and lots of pepper.
—
Grissini (p.16) served in a glass.
—
Wedges of hard-boiled egg with flavoured salt.

* * *

Martini Olives

There are never enough olives in a martini – here's the solution.

Makes 2 cups (500 ml)

* * *

2 cups (500 ml)
green olives

—

Vodka or gin

—

White vermouth (Martini,
Cinzano or Noilly Prat)

—

A few strips of lemon zest

* * *

Drain and rinse olives and pat dry.

—

In a bowl, mix the vodka, a few
dashes of vermouth to taste,
and lemon zest.

—

Add the olives and refrigerate for
at least 1 hour.

* * *

Black Olive Spread

With a glass of rosé, you'll feel like you're in Provence.
This quick spread improves when prepared a few hours in advance.

Makes 1 cup (250 ml)

* * *

1 cup (250 ml)
pitted black olives*

—

1 tsp (5 ml)
finely grated orange zest

—

1 tbsp (15 ml)
orange juice

—

1 tsp (5 ml)
crushed or ground
fennel seeds

—

3 tbsp (45 ml)
olive oil

—

Freshly ground black pepper

* * *

Place pitted olives, orange zest and
juice, fennel seeds and oil in a food
processor. Pulse until coarsely chopped.
Avoid puréeing mixture. Add pepper.

—

Pour into a bowl and refrigerate.

* * *

*To pit olives, place them in a plastic bag and
crush them with a small saucepan or soup can,
or just use an olive pitter.
To draw the salt out, place pitted olives in a bowl,
cover them with boiling water and let them sit for
a few minutes. Rinse under cold water and pat dry
using paper towels.

Serve
This tapenade is delicious on
croutons or vegetables (fennel or
celery), in sandwiches, on cold or hot
pasta, or as a garnish on a mozzarella-
and-tomato salad.

Note
This spread can be made using a
knife or mezzaluna. Dice the olives,
place in a bowl and add the rest of
the ingredients. Mix.

Store
Refrigerate for up to 3 weeks.

Grissini

*Delicious with cheese,
appetizers and soups.*

Makes 24 grissini

* * *

1 lb (500 g)
ball of commercial pizza dough*
or see recipe (p. 103)

—

Plenty of olive oil

—

Sesame, poppy or
fennel seeds, dried rosemary or
oregano, paprika

—

Coarse salt

* * *

Preheat oven to 400°F (200°C).

—

Divide dough in half.

—

On a lightly floured work area,
roll out each piece of dough into a
5- x 12-in (12.5 x 30 cm) rectangle.

—

Sprinkle with selected seeds,
herbs or spices and roll again
to press flavourings into dough.

—

Cut dough into 3/4–in (2 cm)
strips with a knife or pizza wheel.
The breadsticks should be of equal
size for uniform cooking.

—

Roll dough strips between
fingers to make rounded sticks.

—

Place breadsticks on an oiled baking
sheet and coat generously with oil.

Sprinkle with coarse salt and twist,
if desired.

—

Cook in centre of oven for about
15 minutes or until the grissini are dry
and golden brown.

—

Place baking sheet on counter and
let the grissini dry before handling.

* * *

*If the dough is frozen, brush it with oil and place
it in a bowl. Cover with a damp towel and let thaw
in the refrigerator overnight or on the counter for
at least 6 hours.

Smoked Salmon Mousse

A recipe by Daniel Pinard.
Quite simply, smoked salmon blended with cream into a mousse.
The rest is a matter of taste.

/ 018

Makes 1 cup (250 ml)

* * *

5 oz (150 g)
smoked salmon

—

1 tsp (5 ml)
prepared horseradish

—

1 tsp (5 ml)
finely grated lemon zest

—

1 tsp (5 ml)
lemon juice

—

5 tbsp (75 ml)
35% cream

—

1 tbsp (15 ml)
finely chopped chives

—

Freshly ground black pepper

* * *

Place salmon, horseradish and lemon zest and juice in food processor.

—

Pulse to chop coarsely.

—

Still pulsing, add cream a little at a time to obtain a spread-like consistency.

—

Transfer to a bowl. Stir in chives; add pepper to taste.

* * *

Serve
Garnish with a few sprigs
of chives or a few capers.

—

Spread onto croutons.

—

Spoon into an endive leaf and top
with a few trout or salmon eggs.

—

Spoon onto thick, slightly hollowed-
out cucumber slices.

—

Spread on toasted bagel halves.

Chicken Liver Mousse with Figs

This delicious hors d'oeuvre mousse may also serve as an appetizer in individual ramekins. It can be prepared in advance to take to a party or offer as a gift.

Makes 2 1/2 cups (625 ml)

* * *

12 oz (350 g)
chicken livers, trimmed

—

1 1/2 tbsp (25 ml)
white wine vinegar
or cider vinegar

—

3/4 lb (350 g)
cold butter

—

3 tbsp (45 ml)
fortified wine (port, Madeira
or sherry, according to taste)

—

3/4 tsp (4 ml) salt

—

Freshly ground black pepper

—

1/4 tsp (1 ml)
ground allspice

—

1/2 cup (125 ml)
dried figs, diced
and steeped for 20 minutes
in port or other fortified wine

* * *

<u>In a saucepan</u>, cover chicken livers with cold water and add vinegar.

—

<u>Poach</u> over medium-low heat, just below boiling point, for approximately 5 minutes.

—

<u>Remove</u> from heat, drain livers and pat dry with paper towels. Place livers, butter, wine, salt, pepper and allspice in food processor and process to a fine purée. Scrape the sides of the bowl often.

—

<u>Stir</u> in figs.

—

<u>Pour</u> mixture into a bowl or, in small portions, into ramekins.

* * *

Serve
With slices of
toasted brioche

—

With Crostini (p. 172)

—

With apple slices

Variation
Soak figs in
apple juice
and omit alcohol.

Store
Refrigerate for up to a week.
The mousse may also be frozen,
then thawed in the refrigerator
before use.

— Soups —
and Appetizers

* * *

Roasted Leeks with Mint

*Chef Jacques Robert made this recipe on my TV show
and we immediately adopted it.*

Serves 4

* * *

4 small or medium leeks,
trimmed and cut in half lengthwise
but still attached at the base

—

40 to 60 fresh mint leaves

—

Juice of 1/2 lemon

—

Salt and freshly ground pepper

—

1 tbsp (15 ml) sugar

—

1/2 cup (125 ml)
grated Parmesan cheese

* * *

Preheat oven to 400°F (200°C).
Oil a baking sheet.

—

Blanch leeks in salted
boiling water for approximately
2 minutes or until tender.

—

Stop the cooking process by plunging
leeks into a bowl of ice water.

—

Arrange leeks on baking sheet.

—

Insert 5 mint leaves between
the leaves of each half-leek.

—

Sprinkle with a little lemon juice.
Season to taste with salt and pepper.

—

Sprinkle lightly with sugar.

—

Sprinkle with Parmesan cheese
and bake for 5 minutes or until
Parmesan is lightly golden.

* * *

Roasted Asparagus with Parmesan

* * *

Grill asparagus (p. 118) and,
5 minutes before end of cooking time,
sprinkle with grated Parmesan cheese;
grill until melted.

* * *

Peppers à la Piemontaise

*An Italian classic that is usually
garnished with anchovy fillets, yet offers all kinds of possibilities.
Also makes a delicious, attractive side dish.*

Serves 4

* * *

4 plum tomatoes
or 2 regular tomatoes

—

2 orange or yellow bell peppers

—

Plenty of olive oil

—

Salt and freshly ground pepper

—

Crushed garlic
(optional)

* * *

Garnishes, as desired

—

Oregano

—

Basil

—

Pesto

—

Salsa verde

—

Anchovies, cut
in half lengthwise
(decrease salt if
using anchovies)

* * *

Preheat oven to 350°F (180°C).

—

Peel, halve and seed tomatoes
(p. 179).

—

Cut peppers in half lengthwise
through stem. Remove seeds and
brush insides generously with olive
oil. Sprinkle with salt and pepper, add
garlic (if using) and selected garnish.

—

Oil a baking sheet or dish large
enough to hold peppers; add peppers.

—

Place two tomato halves into each
pepper half and sprinkle with salt
and pepper again. Drizzle with oil.

—

Cover with aluminum foil.

—

Cook for 45 minutes, uncover and
cook for another 45 minutes.

* * *

Serve
Hot or at room temperature.

Variation
*Set roasted peppers aside at
room temperature. Place a few
slices of mozzarella on each
plate, drizzle with olive oil and a few
drops of wine vinegar, and season
with salt and pepper. Top with a
pepper half and garnish with black
olives, capers or fresh herbs.*

Artichokes à la Provençale

A light entrée with the flavours of the Midi region.
And for me, the fun of eating with my fingers.

Serves 4

* * *

4 medium artichokes

—

1/2 lemon

—

Olive oil

—

1 onion, quartered, or
2 French shallots, halved

—

2 garlic cloves, halved

—

1 bay leaf

—

Handful of fresh thyme
or 2 tsp (10 ml) dried thyme
or herbes de Provence

—

Salt and a few grains of pepper

—

1/2 cup (125 ml) Noilly Prat
or white wine, or 1/4 cup (60 ml)
white wine vinegar

—

Water or chicken stock

* * *

Garnishes

—

Lemon zest

—

Chopped flat-leaf parsley

—

Sprigs of fresh thyme

* * *

To trim artichokes, remove base leaves. If there is a stem, break it off if you like.

—

Trim artichokes back approximately 1 in (2.5 cm). Using scissors, cut off the pointed ends of the leaves, known as bracts. Rub lemon juice on the cut parts as you work.

—

Scoop out the fuzzy centre with a grapefruit spoon or other small spoon. Rub centre with lemon juice. To make things easier, cut the artichokes in half lengthwise.

—

Use a saucepan just large enough to hold the artichokes. Cover the bottom of the pan with a generous amount of olive oil.

—

Place artichokes upright in pan.

—

Add garlic, bay leaf, thyme, salt, pepper, Noilly Prat and enough water or stock to come two-thirds up the sides of the artichokes. Taste and adjust seasoning. The broth should be salty.

—

Simmer, covered, for 20 to 30 minutes. Test the artichokes for doneness by pulling off a few leaves at the base or by pricking the bottom with a fork.

* * *

Serve

Cold or at room temperature

—

Garnished with lemon zest, parsley and thyme

Green Salad with Parmesan Vinaigrette

This vinaigrette, provided by my friend Arline Gélinas,
is delicious over lettuce, tomatoes or roasted vegetables.
I sometimes top this salad with grilled chicken for lunch.

/ 030

Serves 4

* * *

Plenty of arugula, baby spinach
or other seasonal greens,
washed and spun dry

* * *

Parmesan Vinaigrette

—

1/2 cup (125 ml)
olive oil

—

1/4 cup (60 ml)
grated Parmesan cheese

—

1 tsp (5 ml)
lemon juice

—

2 tsp (10 ml)
white wine vinegar

—

Salt and freshly ground pepper

* * *

Garnishes

—

Onion wedges or roasted
cipollini onions (p. 118)

—

Croutons (p. 172)

—

Shaved Parmigiano-Reggiano
or grana Padano (p. 178)

—

12 thin slices bresaola
or Grisons dried meats

—

4 thin slices raw prosciutto or
Prosciutto Chips (recipe, right)

* * *

In a blender, mix olive oil, Parmesan,
lemon juice and vinegar. Add a little
water, a spoonful at a time, as needed
to thin sauce.

—

Season with salt and pepper to taste.

—

In a large bowl, toss arugula
with vinaigrette, reserving extra
vinaigrette in the refrigerator.

—

Garnish to taste with one or more
of the suggested garnishes.

* * *

Prosciutto Chips

* * *

Preheat oven to 350°F (180°C).
Arrange prosciutto slices on a baking
sheet and cook for 15 minutes.

—

If prosciutto chips don't crisp as they
cool, put them back in the oven for a
few minutes more.

—

Once cooled, prosciutto chips keep
in the refrigerator for several days.

* * *

Tomato-Mango Salad

This quickly became a classic, and with good reason!

Serves 4

* * *

3 red tomatoes,
quartered, or 2 cups (500 ml)
grape tomatoes, halved

—

2 peeled mangoes*,
quartered

—

White wine or other vinegar
(optional)

—

Olive oil

—

Salt and freshly ground pepper

—

Curry powder

—

Basil or coriander leaves,
or chives, minced, to taste

* * *

<u>On a platter</u> or in a salad bowl,
arrange tomatoes and mangoes.

—

<u>Drizzle</u> with a little white wine vinegar
and olive oil and season with salt and
pepper to taste.

—

<u>Sprinkle</u> with a pinch of curry
powder or more to taste. Mix.

—

<u>Garnish</u> with selected herb.

* * *

*Peel mango with a sharp knife or
vegetable peeler.
Cut mango in half by slicing it as close
as possible to the pit.

Braised Beet Salad

*Makes a good appetizer,
or serve alongside salmon or a soufflé.*

/ 034

Serves 4

* * *

4 medium raw beets,
peeled and cubed or quartered

—

1/2 cup (125 ml)
water

—

1/4 cup (60 ml) thinly sliced
French shallot

—

Salt

—

1 tbsp (15 ml)
or more sherry or other
wine vinegar

—

2 tbsp (30 ml) olive oil

Salt and freshly ground pepper

* * *

Garnishes

—

Watercress, niçoise, arugula,
mesclun or other seasonal greens

—

Olive oil, salt and freshly
ground pepper

* * *

In a saucepan, cook beets with water,
shallot and pinch of salt, covered,
for 15 minutes.

—

Drain beets, reserving cooking liquid.

Whisk vinegar, olive oil, salt and
pepper into reserved liquid.

—

Coat beets with vinaigrette.

* * *

*Serve
At room temperature on selected
greens and drizzle with olive oil,
if desired.*

*Variations
For a more robust appetizer,
add a few slices of smoked salmon
or crumble in a little blue cheese.*

—

*Crush a few coriander
or cumin seeds with a mortar and
pestle and add while braising beets.*

Japanese Watercress Salad

*This salad can serve as a base
for an Asian-inspired meal (p. 184).*

Serves 4

* * *

Vinaigrette

—

2 tbsp (30 ml)
rice vinegar

—

2 tbsp (30 ml)
soy sauce

—

1/4 cup (60 ml) olive oil

—

1/2 to 1 tsp (2 to 5 ml)
maple syrup or brown sugar

—

A few drops
of sesame oil (optional)

* * *

Watercress
or baby spinach

—

Grated carrot (optional)

—

Sautéed Shrimp and Scallops
(optional)

* * *

Garnish

—

Sesame seeds
or minced coriander, to taste

* * *

In a large bowl, mix vinegar, soy sauce, olive oil, maple syrup and sesame oil thoroughly.

—

Place watercress, carrots (if using), and seafood (if using), on vinaigrette without tossing. —

Just before serving, toss lightly to coat vegetables with vinaigrette. Garnish with sesame seeds.

* * *

*Serve
With Sautéed Shrimp
and Scallops (below), or alongside
grilled pork or fish.*

Sautéed Shrimp and Scallops

* * *

To sauté shrimp and scallops, dry them carefully with paper towels before cooking them in a little oil over high heat.

—

Cook just until seafood changes colour, no more. Add salt and pepper to taste. You can also add chopped garlic and red pepper flakes. Avoid overcooking, as this will make the seafood rubbery.

* * *

Parmesan, Mushroom and Fennel Salad

So simple and fresh. Bring out your good olive oil.

Serves 4

* * *

2 portobello mushrooms, sliced

—

2 tbsp (30 ml)
olive oil

—

Salt and freshly ground pepper

—

2 tbsp (30 ml)
lemon juice

—

5 tbsp (75 ml)
olive oil

—

2 fennel bulbs,
trimmed (p. 173)

—

1/4 cup (60 ml) shaved Parmigiano-
Reggiano or grana Padano

* * *

Preheat oven to 375°F
(190°C).

—

Arrange mushroom slices on
a lightly oiled baking sheet.
Brush with oil and sprinkle with
salt and pepper.

—

Bake for 12 minutes, turning
mushrooms halfway through.

—

In a small bowl, combine lemon juice
and olive oil.

—

Thinly slice fennel with mandoline or
chef's knife.

On a large plate, fan out fennel slices.
Place mushroom slices on fennel and
garnish with cheese shavings. For tips
on shaving cheese, see p. 178.

—

Drizzle vinaigrette over all.
Season with salt and pepper to taste.

* * *

*Serve
Immediately.*

*Variation
Garnish with Prosciutto
Chips (p. 30), crumbled,
and cheese shavings.*

Apple and Fennel Salad

Yes, I have a weak spot for fennel!

Serves 4

* * *

2 fennel bulbs, trimmed (p. 173)

—

1 or 2 firm apples,
seeded and thinly sliced

—

5 tbsp (75 ml) Lemon Oil (p. 176),
or 5 tbsp (75 ml) olive oil and
2 tbsp (30 ml) lemon juice

—

Salt and freshly
ground pepper to taste

—

Shaved Parmigiano-Reggiano
or grana Padano (p. 178)

* * *

Thinly slice fennel with mandoline
or chef's knife.

—

On a large plate, fan out fennel
slices. Place apple slices on fennel.

—

Drizzle with lemon oil.

—

Season with salt and pepper to taste
and garnish with Parmesan shavings.

* * *

*Variation
The best-known of all,
the one my grandmother used to
make: thinly sliced fennel bulbs,
peeled orange slices or segments
with their juices, olive oil, salt and
freshly ground pepper.*

Dried Duck Breasts

Making your own "deli meats" is satisfying.
Thanks again to Jacques Robert.

12 appetizer portions

* * *

2 duck breasts*,
about 1 lb (500 g) each

—

Plenty of
coarse salt

—

Cracked pepper

—

Fresh thyme
(optional)

* * *

<u>Cover</u> duck breasts with salt.

—

<u>Refrigerate</u> for 36 hours.

—

<u>Remove</u> duck breasts from salt,
rinse with cold water and pat dry
thoroughly.

—

<u>Sprinkle</u> pepper on meat side of
breasts. Place thyme between them
and tie together securely with string.

—

<u>Wrap</u> meat in a dish towel and let
cure in refrigerator for 10 days.

* * *

Before serving
Scrape off pepper and
discard thyme. Trim excess fat,
leaving only a thin layer. Slice very
thinly. To slice thinly, place between
two sheets of waxed or parchment
paper and pound with a rolling pin,
then slice using a very sharp knife.

Serve
With a salad
—
With fresh fruit wedges
(melon, figs, pears, etc.)
—
With drinks, along with olives,
Grissini (p. 16), etc.

Store
In the refrigerator for 2 to 3 weeks,
completely wrapped in a dish towel.
—
You can also ask
your butcher to slice the
duck breasts and vacuum-pack
them in small batches.

*As with any raw meat, ensure that utensils
and work area are very clean.

Oysters

I can't wait for oyster season!

* * *

When purchasing, select oysters that are tightly closed and do not sound hollow when tapped with a stick.

—

Store oysters, uncleaned, with the flat side up so that the mollusk lies in its liquor. Avoid storing oysters in a plastic bag. Place oysters in a bowl and cover them with a damp towel, which you will redampen as needed. Don't cover the bowl with plastic wrap, as this prevents the oysters from breathing. Oysters will keep for one to four weeks in the refrigerator, depending on the variety.

—

Before serving, scrub oysters under cold running water. Do not soak.

—

Prepare a platter by filling it with coarse salt or crushed ice. Sink oysters into salt or ice.

* * *

Cold Oysters

* * *

A selection of garnishes is set out on the table and guests help themselves to whatever they like:

_ Lime or lemon quarters
_ My own concoction: equal parts lime juice and rice vinegar, freshly grated ginger and finely diced French shallot
_ Vodka in a shot glass
_ Commercial hot sauces

* * *

Variations

Serve with virgin or regular Bloody Mary shooters, garnished with a stalk of celery. For the sake of nostalgia, include some chili sauce, prepared horseradish and lime juice.

Top each oyster with a slice of hot grilled sausage (chorizo or spicy sausage) and lime or lemon wedges.

Hot Oysters

* * *

Oysters with Almond Butter Gratin: Mix equal parts ground roasted almonds and softened butter. Add a little minced French shallot and sprinkle this mixture over oysters. Place on a baking sheet filled with coarse salt and cook for 5 minutes at 425°F (220°C). Brown under broiler for 1 to 2 minutes.

* * *

Minestrone

This is tops in comfort food.
For vegetable soup, you can trust Biaggio "Nino" Marcone of the Jean-Talon Market in Montreal.
After all, he does know a thing or two about vegetables!

Serves 8 to 10

* * *

Dried white or freshly
picked romano beans

—

2 bay leaves

—

1 celery root, peeled and cubed

—

3 potatoes, peeled and cubed

—

1/2 head kale, coarsely chopped

—

1 onion, chopped

—

4 carrots, peeled

—

Small artichokes, about 8,
hearts trimmed (optional)

—

2 pieces Parmesan rind

—

10 cups (2.5 l)
hot chicken stock

—

Salt and freshly ground pepper

—

2 or 3 yellow or green
zucchini, cubed

* * *

Garnishes

—

Olive oil

—

Grated Parmesan

—

Pesto

* * *

In a large saucepan, cover dried
beans with plenty of cold water and
add bay leaves.

—

Cook for 40 to 50 minutes or until
beans are almost tender. Salt water
halfway through cooking.
Drain beans.

—

Return beans to pan and add celery
root, potatoes, kale, onion, carrots,
artichokes (if using) and Parmesan
rind.

—

Add stock and season to taste with
salt and pepper.

—

Simmer for approximately 20 minutes.

—

Add zucchini and cook for another
5 minutes.

—

Before serving, remove Parmesan
rind.

* * *

Serve
Let guests drizzle olive oil
and sprinkle Parmesan
over their soup, or add a spoonful
of pesto to it.

Variations
Dried beans can be replaced by
canned white beans. Just drain and
rinse beans and add to soup at the
same time as zucchini.

—

To cook freshly picked romano beans,
cook them in chicken stock with 2 bay
leaves, a healthy dash of olive oil and
6 cherry tomatoes. Cook until beans
are almost tender.

Store
In serving-size portions
in the freezer.

Stracciatella

*My mother's stracciatella is the best in the world
because her broth is, naturally, the best in the world!*

Serves 4

* * *

4 cups (1 l) chicken stock

—

1 egg
(for soup with pasta)
or 2 eggs
(for soup without pasta)

—

Freshly ground pepper

—

Freshly grated nutmeg, to taste

—

1 rounded tbsp (15 ml) grated
Parmesan, or more to taste

—

Cooked short pasta: risoni, orzo,
anchellini, etc. (optional)

—

Chopped parsley

* * *

<u>In a large saucepan</u>, bring stock
to a boil.

—

<u>In a bowl,</u> beat together eggs,
pepper, nutmeg and Parmesan.

—

<u>Reduce</u> heat until stock is simmering;
add egg mixture. When the mixture
begins to coagulate, stir with a fork
to break up.

—

<u>Before serving</u>, add short pasta
(if using) and chopped parsley.

* * *

Chinese Egg Drop Soup

Serves 4

* * *

4 cups (1 l) chicken stock

—

3 tbsp (45 ml) soy sauce

—

2 tsp (10 ml) diced fresh ginger

* * *

Vegetables, to taste

—

Sliced fresh mushrooms, shredded
napa cabbage, julienned snow peas,
baby spinach and/or bean sprouts

* * *

2 eggs

—

1/2 cup (125 ml) minced green onion

* * *

<u>In a medium saucepan</u>, combine
stock, soy sauce and ginger and bring
to a boil.

—

<u>Add</u> selected vegetables, reduce heat
and simmer gently for 2 minutes.

—

<u>In a small bowl</u>, beat eggs with a fork.

<u>Blend</u> in eggs. When eggs begin to
coagulate, stir with a fork.

—

<u>Garnish</u> with green onion and serve
immediately.

—

<u>You can also season</u> the soup with
a few drops of sesame oil.

* * *

Butternut Squash Soup

Roasting the squash means you can skip the peeling step — and the flavour is more concentrated.
There are several ways to serve this soup. It's a matter of preference.

Serves 6

* * *

1 butternut squash,
2 lb (1 kg)

—

4 garlic cloves,
unpeeled

—

3 tbsp (45 ml)
olive oil

—

Salt and freshly ground pepper

—

1 large onion
or 6 French shallots, minced

—

3 tbsp (45 ml) butter

—

2 tbsp (30 ml)
finely diced fresh ginger

—

2 tsp (10 ml)
mild curry powder

—

4 cups (1 l)
chicken or vegetable stock

—

* * *

Garnish

—

Plain yogurt
and lime wedges

* * *

Cut squash in half. This is easier
to do with a large knife and mallet.
Remove seeds.

—

Preheat oven to 375°F (190°C).

—

Line a baking sheet with foil or
parchment paper.

—

Brush squash and garlic cloves with
oil and season with salt and pepper.
Place squash halves on baking sheet,
cut side down. Place garlic cloves
under squash.

—

Cook in centre of oven for 45 minutes
or until flesh is tender.

—

Let cool for 10 minutes before peeling
squash halves and garlic. Set aside.

—

In a soup pot over medium heat,
fry onion in butter until soft, about
10 minutes, stirring often.

—

Add ginger and curry. Cook for
1 minute.

—

Add squash, garlic and stock. Bring
to a boil over high heat, reduce heat
and let simmer, uncovered, for
10 minutes.

—

Purée soup in blender. Thin with stock
or water as needed.

—

Heat through.

* * *

Serve
Garnished with yogurt and
lime wedges.

Variations
Replace yogurt with coconut milk at
the end of cooking, and lime wedges
with shredded spinach. Garnish soup
with sliced roasted almonds.

—

Pour soup into heated deep bowl.
In centre, place seared shrimp or
scallops. Garnish with chives or a
drizzle of flavoured oil.

Mushroom Stock

Here is a light, refined appetizer with delicious flavour…
practically a lifesaver!

/ 048

Makes 4 cups (1 l)

* * *

6 cups (1.5 l)
low-sodium chicken
or vegetable stock

—

2 or 3 French shallots, minced

—

1/2 oz (15 g)
dried porcini mushrooms

—

1/4 tsp (1 ml) dried thyme,
or more to taste, or 1 sprig
fresh thyme

—

Salt and freshly ground pepper

* * *

<u>In a soup pot</u>, bring stock, shallots, porcini mushrooms and thyme to a boil. Simmer for 15 to 20 minutes, uncovered, or until reduced to 4 cups (1 l). Season with salt and pepper to taste. Cool and strain stock.

* * *

Serve
Add some cheese or cooked mushroom ravioli or tortellini pasta to hot stock. Garnish with flat-leaf parsley or watercress leaves.

—

Add some thinly sliced cremini or shiitake mushrooms (without stems), or diced chives and enoki mushrooms to hot stock.

Mushroom Cappuccino

Fools the eye, not the taste buds!

Serves 4

* * *

1 onion, finely diced

—

1 leek, trimmed
and finely diced

—

2 tbsp (30 ml) butter

—

1 lb (500 g)
mushrooms, sliced

—

1 small potato,
peeled and quartered

—

Salt and freshly ground pepper

—

1 tbsp (15 ml)
fresh thyme or 1 tsp (5 ml)
dried thyme

—

1/3 to 1/2 oz (10 to 15 g)
dried porcini mushrooms, ground*
(optional)

—

3 cups (750 ml)
chicken stock

—

1 cup (250 ml)
35% cream

* * *

In a soup pot, fry onion and leek in
butter over low heat until tender.

—

Add mushrooms, increase heat
and cook until juices evaporate.

—

Add potato, season to taste with salt
and pepper, and add thyme.

—

Set aside 1 tbsp (15 ml) ground
porcini mushrooms.

—

Add remaining ground porcini
mushrooms and stock to pot.

—

Bring to a boil, reduce heat and
simmer, half-covered, for 15 minutes.

—

A few minutes before serving,
add 1/2 cup (125 ml) of the cream.

—

In blender, purée soup. Thin as needed
with stock or water.

—

Keep warm.

—

Whip remaining cream.

* * *

Serve

*Pour soup into 4 mugs. Cover
each portion with whipped cream to
imitate the foam on a cappuccino.
Sprinkle remaining ground porcini
mushrooms onto cream.*

Variation

*Replace cream with heated skim
or 2% milk. Using a cappuccino
whisk, foam milk.*

*Grind porcini mushrooms in a coffee grinder.
To clean grinder, put 2 tbsp (30 ml) coarse salt
into grinder and activate, shaking grinder at the
same time. Discard salt and wipe grinder clean
with a damp towel. Let dry.

— Main Dishes —

* * *

Ham and Egg Ramekins

A weekend brunch solution.

Serves 6

* * *

6 slices sandwich bread,
crusts removed

—

Butter

—

6 slices old-fashioned ham,
5 in (12.5 cm) in diameter

—

6 large eggs

—

Salt and freshly ground pepper

* * *

Garnishes, to taste

(optional)

—

Baby spinach

—

Sliced mushrooms
sautéed in butter

* * *

Preheat oven to 350°F (180°C).

—

With a rolling pin, flatten bread
slices as thinly as possible.

—

Butter one side of each slice and
place, buttered side down, in muffin
tins. Top with ham slices.

—

If desired, add selected garnish.
Top with 1 egg. Season with salt
and pepper to taste.

—

Bake in oven for 20 to 25 minutes,
until eggs are done.

* * *

Serve
Alongside a baby spinach,
mesclun or seasonal green salad

—

With tomato salsa

—

With tomatoes drizzled
with olive oil and garnished
with fresh herbs

Variation
Omit bread

Cheese Soufflés

*Pretty and delicious. I tasted this recipe at a brunch
held by my friend Stéphan Boucher. I like the fact that they can be made ahead of time;
just reheat whenever you like, at any time of day.*

Serves 6

* * *

1 tbsp (15 ml)
butter, melted

—

2 tbsp (30 ml)
grated Parmesan, or
1/4 cup (60 ml) walnuts or
pecans, roasted and ground

—

3 tbsp (45 ml)
butter

—

1/4 cup (60 ml)
all-purpose flour

—

1 cup (250 ml) milk

—

1 cup (250 ml)
shredded Gruyère or
old Cheddar cheese

—

4 eggs, separated

—

1/3 cup (80 ml)
fresh herbs (chives, parsley,
dill, basil), chopped, or to taste

—

Salt and freshly ground pepper

* * *

Preheat oven to 350°F (180°C).
Brush six 3/4-cup (180 ml) ramekins
with melted butter and sprinkle with
grated Parmesan or ground nuts.

—

In a small saucepan, melt butter.
Add flour and cook for 1 minute,
stirring.

—

Whisk in milk. Bring to a boil,
whisking constantly. Cook for
3 minutes.

—

Blend in cheese and stir until melted.
Remove from heat; let cool.

—

Add egg yolks, selected herbs, and
salt and pepper to taste. Whisk
thoroughly.

—

In a bowl, using an electric mixer,
beat egg whites with a pinch of salt
until firm. Add 1/3 of the egg whites
to the cheese mixture, folding in to
expand mixture.

—

Pour in remaining egg whites and
fold in with spatula. Fill ramekins
evenly. Place ramekins in a baking
dish; fill with boiling water halfway
up sides of ramekins.

—

Bake for 25 minutes.

Run a knife blade around each soufflé
and carefully remove from ramekin.

—

Serve immediately.

—

If soufflés are not served immediately,
place them on a buttered or
parchment-lined baking sheet.

—

The soufflés can then be refrigerated
and reheated in the oven for
10 minutes at 425°F (220°C).

* * *

Serve

*Alongside Roasted Asparagus
(p. 118) and/or a green salad*

—

With Braised Beet Salad (p. 34)

Chèvre Soufflés

* * *

Replace Gruyère or Cheddar cheese
with 1 cup (250 ml) crumbled fresh
goat cheese log.

* * *

Spice-Rubbed Salmon

*The crunch and smell of the spice
rub with the tenderness of the salmon—a consummate success!
The only skill required is heat control, to avoid burning the spices.*

Serves 4

* * *

2 tbsp (30 ml)
coriander seeds

—

2 tbsp (30 ml)
mustard seeds

—

1 tbsp (15 ml)
white or maple sugar
(optional)

—

2 tsp (10 ml) sea salt

—

1/2 tsp (2 ml)
cracked pepper

—

4 salmon fillets,
5 oz (150 g) each

—

2 tbsp (30 ml)
olive oil, or
1 tbsp (15 ml) each olive oil
and butter

* * *

Preheat oven to 450°F (230°C).

—

Coarsely grind coriander and mustard
seeds (or your own blend of spices)
in a coffee grinder or with a mortar
and pestle, or place in a resealable
plastic bag and crush with the bottom
of a small heavy pan.

—

Mix spices, sugar, salt and pepper
on a plate.

—

Coat salmon with spice mixture
and let spices infuse the fish for a
few minutes.

—

In a nonstick frying pan, heat oil
over medium heat.

—

Add fish and brown for approximately
1 minute. Take care to not burn
the spice crust.

Turn salmon pieces over and
sear other side.

—

Wrap aluminum foil around pan
handle and bake in oven for 5 to
8 minutes, just long enough for the
centre of the fillet to stay nice and
pink.

* * *

*Serve
Immediately, with
Mashed Potatoes with
Arugula (p. 122) and
Braised Beet Salad (p. 34)*

—

*With a green or
seasonal salad*

—

*With Warm
Potato Salad (p. 124)*

Asian-Style Salmon Patties

Is there room for yet another salmon recipe? You bet!

Serves 4

* * *

1 1/3 lb (600 g) fresh salmon,
skinned and boned

—

4 to 6 green onions, minced,
or 1/4 cup (60 ml) chives, snipped

—

2 tbsp (30 ml)
grated fresh ginger,
or 1 tbsp (15 ml)
marinated ginger, minced

—

Pinch cayenne pepper
or sambal oelek

—

Salt and freshly ground pepper

—

Olive oil for cooking

* * *

Place half of the salmon in food processor and pulse until coarsely chopped, or chop with a knife. Do not purée. Transfer to bowl.

—

Chop remaining salmon in the same manner and add this to the first part, along with green onions, ginger, cayenne, salt and pepper.

—

Mix gently.

—

Refrigerate for a few hours, if desired.

—

Divide into four or eight equal parts and form slightly flattened balls.

Cook patties in a spoonful of oil in a nonstick pan over medium-high heat for 3 minutes per side. Turn only once and take care not to overcook.

* * *

Serve
With Japanese Watercress
Salad (p. 35), spinach or
bok choy (p. 114)

—

Variation
To make a burger,
spread mayonnaise flavoured with
a pinch of wasabi onto a hamburger
bun and garnish with slices of
cucumber or marinated ginger.

Salmon Patties Dijonnaise

Serves 4

* * *

1 1/3 lb (600 g) fresh salmon,
skinned and boned

—

4 green onions, minced,
or 1/4 cup (60 ml) chives, snipped

—

2 tbsp (30 ml) Meaux
or Dijon mustard

—

Paprika or Espelette pepper, to taste

—

Salt and freshly ground pepper

—

1 tbsp (15 ml) olive oil
or 1 1/2 tsp (7 ml) each butter
and olive oil for cooking

* * *

Proceed as described above, modifying ingredients.

* * *

Serve
With Warm Potato Salad (p. 124)

—

Variation
To make a burger, garnish with
lettuce and mayonnaise flavoured
with lemon juice and zest.

Catch of the Day with Orange Sauce

A delightful blend of juicy orange, fish and a green vegetable.
Ready in minutes! The sauce, a variation on beurre blanc,
is prepared while the fish is cooking.

Serves 4

* * *

4 fresh fish fillets,
according to availability,
about 5 oz (150 g) each

—

Olive oil

—

Salt and freshly ground pepper

—

Orange Sauce

—

1 tbsp (15 ml)
orange zest

—

1/2 cup (125 ml)
orange juice

—

2 tbsp (30 ml)
lemon juice or Pernod

—

1/2 cup (125 ml)
cold butter, cubed

* * *

Preheat oven to 425°F (220°C).

—

Line a baking sheet with parchment
paper or aluminum foil.

—

Make sure that the ingredients for the
sauce are prepared.

—

Coat fish with oil and season with
salt and pepper.

—

Cook fish in centre of oven, 5 to
7 minutes for thin fillets, 10 minutes
for thick fillets.

—

While fish is cooking, prepare sauce.
Pour orange zest and juice and lemon
juice into a small saucepan.

—

Bring to a boil and reduce for
1 minute over high heat. Season with
salt and pepper to taste.

Add butter cubes, a few at a time,
whisking between each addition.

—

Ladle immediately over fish.

* * *

Serve
With bok choy or
a green vegetable of your choice,
along with Basmati Rice (p. 128)
or a Mash (p. 122 and 123).

Variation
This orange sauce is perfect
with asparagus as well.

Pan-Fried Shrimp with Ginger Emulsion

*Chef Fabrice Coutanceau introduced me to this sauce,
which he serves with lobster.
I've use it over vegetables, rice, grilled fish and shrimp.*

Serves 4

* * *

Ginger Emulsion

—

1/4 cup (60 ml)
chicken stock

—

1 tbsp (15 ml)
tamari or soy sauce

—

1 tbsp (15 ml)
sherry vinegar or rice vinegar

—

2 tbsp (30 ml)
fresh ginger, chopped

—

1/4 cup (60 ml)
olive oil

* * *

4 medium leeks, trimmed and
thoroughly cleaned

—

5 tbsp (75 ml)
olive oil

—

Salt and freshly ground pepper

—

1 1/2 lb (650 g)
large shrimp, peeled

—

1 tsp (5 ml) crushed red pepper or
1 chili pepper, finely diced

* * *

Prepare the ginger emulsion first.
In a small saucepan, bring chicken
stock, tamari, vinegar and ginger
to a boil.

—

Pour mixture into blender and blend.
Pour in oil in a thin stream until sauce
emulsifies. Set aside.

—

Preheat oven to 400°F (200°C).

—

Blanch leeks in salted boiling water
for 2 minutes.

—

Halt the cooking process by plunging
leeks into a bowl of ice water. Drain
and cut leeks in half crosswise, then
lengthwise.

—

Arrange leeks in a single layer on a
baking sheet. Pour 3 tbsp (45 ml) of
the olive oil over leeks and season
with salt and pepper to taste.

—

Bake in oven for 15 minutes, turning
twice. The leeks are ready when the
ends are golden brown. Keep warm.

—

While leeks are cooking, heat
remaining oil in a large frying pan
over high heat. Sauté shrimp for
3 to 5 minutes, until they colour.
At the end of cooking, season with
salt and pepper, and add crushed
red pepper.

* * *

Serve
*Place leeks on heated plates and top
with shrimp and sauce.*

Variation
*Replace leeks with bok choy or
another green vegetable and serve
with Basmati Rice (p. 128).*

/ 065

Hearty Asian Chicken Soup

Hot, uplifting, comforting—all in one bowl.

Serves 4

* * *

7 oz (200 g)
Chinese egg noodles or soba

—

2 tbsp (30 ml)
soy sauce

—

1 tbsp (15 ml) honey

—

2 garlic cloves, minced

—

4 boneless chicken thighs or
4 oz (120 g) chicken breasts

—

6 cups (1.5 l)
good homemade or commercial
chicken or vegetable stock

—

2 to 3 tbsp (30 to 45 ml)
grated fresh ginger

—

2 tbsp (30 ml) lemongrass*,
minced, or zest of 1 lemon or
2 limes, minced

* * *

Vegetables, to taste

—

Bok choy or
napa cabbage, shredded

—

Cremini (coffee) mushrooms,
minced, or shiitake mushrooms,
stems removed

—

Julienned carrots,
baby spinach or minced
green onion

—

Broccoli, divided into florets

* * *

Preheat oven to 425°F (220°C).

—

Line a baking sheet with
parchment paper or aluminum foil.

—

In a large pan, bring water to a boil
to cook noodles. Remove from heat.

—

In a bowl, mix soy sauce, honey and
half of the garlic. Let chicken
marinate in this mixture for a few
minutes.

—

Place chicken on baking sheet
and bake for 15 minutes or until
cooked. Fold paper over chicken
and keep warm.

—

Cook noodles according to package
directions. Drain and rinse under
cold water. Set aside.

—

In a large pan, bring stock to a
boil and add ginger, lemongrass
and remaining garlic. Simmer for
5 minutes, partially covered.

—

Shortly before serving, add 1 1/2 cups
(375 ml) vegetables per portion to
stock. Cook for a few minutes only,
to keep them crunchy.

—

Shred chicken and keep warm.

—

Transfer noodles to a strainer and
plunge them into boiling soup for
1 minute to reheat.

* * *

Before serving
Divide noodles into large bowls and
cover with vegetables. Top with
chicken pieces and pour in hot stock.

Serve
With an assortment of condiments,
such as soy or tamari,
sambal oelek, garlic pepper paste
or fresh coriander.

*To trim lemongrass, cut stem 6 in (15 cm)
from the base. Remove the first two or three
exterior layers, reserving only the heart. Dice as
finely as possible with a knife or grind in coffee
grinder. Keep remaining stems to flavour other
stocks and broths. Freezes well.

Cheesy Chicken with Roasted Vegetables

*The chicken cooks alongside the vegetables in this simple,
flavourful and comforting dish.*

/ 068

Serves 4

* * *

Roasted Vegetables

—

4 carrots, peeled and
cut in half lengthwise

—

4 parsnips, peeled and
cut in half lengthwise

—

4 small leeks, thoroughly cleaned
and cut in half lengthwise

—

8 fingerling or baby potatoes

—

4 tbsp (60 ml)
olive oil

—

Salt and freshly ground pepper

* * *

1/2 cup (125 ml)
ricotta cheese

—

1/2 cup (125 ml) herbs,
according to taste (chives, sage,
basil, thyme or rosemary)

—

2 tsp (10 ml)
grated lemon zest

—

Garlic, minced,
to taste

—

Salt and freshly ground pepper

—

4 pieces of chicken with skin
(I prefer legs)

* * *

Preheat oven to 375°F (190°C).
Line one large or two medium baking
sheets with parchment paper or
aluminum foil.

—

Arrange carrots, parsnips, leeks
and potatoes in a single layer on
baking sheet.

—

Pour oil in a thin stream over
the vegetables, then season
generously with salt and pepper.

—

With your hands, coat vegetables
with oil.

—

In a small bowl, mix ricotta, herbs,
lemon zest, garlic, salt and pepper.

—

With your fingers, pull chicken skin
away from flesh, taking care not
to tear skin. Insert approximately
2 tbsp (30 ml) herbed cheese under
the skin of each chicken piece.

—

Place chicken pieces among vegetables
on baking sheet. Sprinkle chicken
with salt and pepper, particularly
the side without cheese.

—

Cook for 45 minutes in centre of oven
or until chicken is golden and well
done. Turn vegetables twice during
cooking and remove them if they are
ready before the chicken.

* * *

Serve

*As is or with Balsamic Vinegar
Sauce (below)*

Note

*If you use a single baking sheet,
place it in the centre of the oven.
If you need to use two baking sheets,
place one in the centre and the other
on the rack below, alternating every
15 minutes and increasing cooking
time slightly.*

Balsamic Vinegar Sauce

* * *

1 cup (250 ml)
low-sodium chicken stock

—

1/3 cup (80 ml) balsamic vinegar

—

3 tbsp (45 ml) cold butter, cubed

* * *

Bring stock and vinegar to a boil
and reduce to 3/4 cup (180 ml).

—

Remove from heat and whisk
in butter.

—

Serve immediately.

* * *

Herbed Chicken

* * *

Omit cheese and bind herb mixture
with a little oil.

* * *

Pancetta Chicken Casserole

A simple party dish.

Serves 4

* * *

1 1/2 lbs (650 g)
boneless chicken thighs
(8 to 12, depending on size)

—

2 tsp (10 ml)
fennel seeds, crushed (optional)

—

1 tbsp (15 ml)
herbes de Provence, or
3 tbsp (45 ml) fresh rosemary or
thyme, finely chopped

—

2 garlic cloves, crushed

—

Zest of 2 lemons, grated

—

3 tbsp (45 ml)
olive oil

—

Salt and freshly ground pepper

—

1 large onion, sliced

—

4 garlic cloves, whole

—

8 to 12 slices of pancetta

—

1/4 cup (60 ml)
chicken stock

—

Juice of 1 lemon

* * *

Preheat oven to 425°F (220°C).

—

On work surface, butterfly boneless
chicken thighs.

—

In a small bowl, combine fennel
seeds, herbs, garlic, lemon zest and
1 tbsp (15 ml) of the olive oil.

—

Spread evenly on chicken pieces,
season with salt and pepper, and
close up meat to create little bundles.

—

Pour half of the remaining oil into a
baking dish.

—

Add onion to dish and coat with oil.
Place chicken and whole garlic
cloves on onion.

—

Place one slice of pancetta on
each chicken bundle.

—

Pour chicken stock and
lemon juice into dish.

—

Cook for 40 to 45 minutes,
uncovered. Halfway through cooking,
add more stock if needed.

* * *

Serve

*With Zucchini-Tomato
Tian (p. 112)*

—

*With flavoured Mashed
Potatoes (p. 122) and Roasted
Cherry Tomatoes (p. 118)*

—

With Pepperonata (p. 120)

Turkey Cutlets Piccata

*There are classics you never tire of — especially
when lemon is involved!*

Serves 4

* * *

4 turkey or chicken cutlets,
5 oz (150 g) each

—

2/3 cup (160 ml) instant or
all-purpose flour

—

Salt and freshly ground pepper

—

4 tbsp (60 ml) cold butter

—

2 tbsp (30 ml) olive oil

—

1/2 cup (125 ml)
white wine or Noilly Prat

—

3/4 cup (180 ml)
chicken stock

—

2 to 3 tbsp (30 to 45 ml)
lemon juice

—

2 tbsp (30 ml) capers, rinsed

—

1/4 cup (60 ml) coarsely chopped
flat-leaf parsley

* * *

Toss cutlets in flour, salt and pepper.

—

In a nonstick pan over high heat,
melt 1 tbsp (15 ml) of the butter in
the same amount of the olive oil until
butter foams.

—

Sear cutlets, two at a time, 1 minute
per side until browned, turning once.

—

Set cutlets aside and keep warm on a
serving platter.

—

Repeat with the remaining two
cutlets.

—

Discard cooking fat and, using a
wooden spoon, deglaze pan with
white wine, taking care to scrape
up brown bits.

—

Pour in stock and reduce by half.

Add lemon juice, capers, parsley and
remaining butter (optional) and stir
constantly until butter is blended
into sauce.

—

Pour sauce over cutlets.

—

You may prepare the cutlets ahead of
time and reheat them in the sauce,
which you can thin by adding a little
stock if necessary.

* * *

Serve
*With pasta topped with herbs or
sun-dried tomato pesto*

—

*With Roasted Green Beans (p. 118) or
other green vegetable (p. 114)*

Variation
*During the holidays, replace
capers with dried cranberries.*

Turkey Breast with Grapefruit

For a large family,
two turkey breasts can marinate in the same amount of brine.
This type of preparation yields a tender, juicy white meat — provided,
of course, that it is not overcooked.

Serves 6

* * *

Brine

—

8 cups (2 l)
cold water

—

1/2 cup (125 ml) salt

—

3 tbsp (45 ml) sugar

—

1 tsp (5 ml)
cracked black pepper

—

2 garlic cloves, crushed

* * *

1 skinless turkey breast,
approximately 2 lbs (1 kg)

—

2 tbsp (30 ml) oil

—

5 French shallots
or 3 small onions, sliced

—

1 tbsp (15 ml)
grated grapefruit zest and
1/2 cup (125 ml)
grapefruit juice

—

1/2 cup (125 ml)
white wine or Noilly Prat

—

1 1/2 cups (375 ml)
chicken stock*

—

1/2 cup (125 ml)
dried cranberries
(optional)

—

2 tbsp (30 ml)
cold butter, cubed

* * *

Pour water, salt, sugar, pepper and garlic into a bowl and mix until salt and sugar are completely dissolved.

—

Add turkey breast to mixture and let brine for 3 hours in refrigerator.

—

Remove turkey from brine and pat dry with paper towels. Tie together with string, if desired.

—

Preheat oven to 350°F (180°C).

—

In a large pan, sear turkey breast in oil, turning to brown all sides. Add shallots.

—

Wrap pan handle with aluminum foil. Cook for 1 hour in centre of oven.

—

Add grapefruit zest and juice, white wine, stock and cranberries (if using).

—

Continue cooking for 15 minutes or until internal temperature of turkey reaches 160°F (70°C).

—

Remove turkey from oven, cover with aluminum foil and let rest for 15 minutes. The internal temperature will rise to 170°F (75°C).

While turkey is resting, reduce cooking juices (without straining) for 2 minutes over high heat.

—

Add cubes of cold butter, one at a time, whisking until incorporated.

—

Slice turkey and serve it in the cooking juices.

* * *

Serve
With Sweet Potato Mash
without the olives (p. 123),
small peas or green beans.

*Chicken stock may be replaced with veal stock or equal parts chicken and veal stock.

Duck and Turkey Pie

A recipe from my friend Michelle Gélinas.
This festive pie takes time but has the huge advantage of being made ahead of time to freeze,
so you can entertain without any last-minute work. Michelle sometimes makes it topped with puff pastry.

/ 076

Serves 10

* * *

4 oz (120 g) lardoons, blanched

—

Duck fat or olive oil

—

1 1/2 lbs (750 g)
boneless turkey, diced
(half a breast)

—

1 lb (500 g) duck, diced
(1 breast)

—

1 onion, finely diced

—

2 garlic cloves, minced

—

2 tbsp (30 ml) flour

—

3/4 cup (180 ml) beef stock

—

1/2 cup (125 ml) dried cranberries

—

1 tsp (5 ml) dried savory

—

1 tsp (5 ml) dried thyme

—

1/2 tsp (2 ml) ground cloves

—

Salt and freshly ground pepper

—

1 1/2 times the recipe
for Pâte Brisée, prepared in
advance (p. 179) or 2 lbs (1 kg)
commercial pâte brisée

—

Coarse salt (optional)

* * *

Glaze

—

1 egg yolk mixed with
1 tbsp (15 ml) cold water

* * *

Preheat oven to 400°F (200°C).

—

In a large pan, brown lardoons in
2 tbsp (30 ml) duck fat for 5 minutes.
Drain on paper towels. Set aside in
a large bowl.

—

Reserve 1/4 cup (60 ml) of cooking
fat in pan.

—

In the same pan, cook turkey
and duck until browned and
cooked through.

—

Drain meat in a strainer and transfer
to bowl with lardoons.

—

In the same pan, render 2 tbsp
(30 ml) duck fat, then sweat onion
and garlic over medium heat.

—

Add flour and cook, stirring,
for 2 minutes over low heat.

—

Add stock, stirring, and simmer
gently for 5 minutes.

—

Pour sauce over meat and
add cranberries, savory, thyme,
cloves, salt and pepper. Blend,
remove from heat and let cool.

On a floured work surface, roll
out half of the dough and fit into
bottom of a deep 10-in (25 cm)
pie plate. Pour filling into pie crust.
Moisten edge of dough.

—

Roll out remaining dough and cover
filling, pressing edges firmly together.
Flute edge of pie. Make an opening
in the centre and cut slits in top of pie
with a knife.

—

Brush with glaze and, if desired,
sprinkle with coarse salt. Bake in
oven for 60 minutes.

* * *

Serve
With Braised
Beet Salad (p. 34), a green salad
and Cranberry Sauce (p. 170)

Store
To freeze pie: Before cooking,
carefully wrap the pie in
plastic wrap, then aluminum foil.
Pie will keep in freezer for up to
3 months. To serve, thaw pie in
refrigerator for 36 hours. Brush with
glaze and bake as directed.

Duck Confit

When you find prepared confit, stock up.
It keeps a long time and can be prepared in multiple ways.
It's a very elegant lifesaver!

Serves 4

* * *

4 pieces of commercial
duck confit

* * *

<u>Preheat</u> oven to 350°F (180°C).

—

<u>Place</u> confit pieces on a baking sheet.
Cover with aluminum foil and heat for
20 minutes or until hot.

—

<u>Before serving</u>, place under grill
for 3 to 4 minutes to crisp skin.

* * *

Serving suggestions

* * *

With Roasted Vegetables
to taste (p. 117 and 118)

—

With a green salad
topped with grapes

—

With Braised Beet Salad (p. 34)

—

Bone confit and serve in a
baking dish, Parmentier-style—that
is, with caramelized onion stuffed
between two layers of
Mashed Potato (p. 122) or
Mashed Celeriac (p. 123), along
with a green salad

—

With Lentil Stew (p. 126)

—

With Japanese Watercress
Salad (p. 35) and
sautéed mushrooms

* * *

Vegetable and Confit Sandwich with Hoisin Sauce

* * *

Tortillas

—

Plenty of hoisin sauce

—

Finely julienned carrot

—

Finely julienned green onion

—

Finely julienned cucumber

—

Very fresh bean sprouts

—

Duck confit, boned and cut into
bite-sized pieces

* * *

<u>Wrap</u> tortillas in a sheet of foil.
Heat for 5 minutes at end of confit
cooking time.

—

<u>Spread</u> a wide band of hoisin
sauce down the centre of a hot
tortilla. Over this band of sauce,
place vegetables and bites of confit.

—

<u>Fold</u> tortilla over filling.

* * *

Asian-Style Pork Tenderloin

*It's not like we're short of pork loin recipes here in Quebec!
In this one, the loins cook alongside the accompanying vegetables,
making this a unique, quick dish for simple gatherings.*

Serves 4

* * *

Marinade
—
3 tbsp (45 ml)
soy sauce or tamari
—
2 tbsp (30 ml)
peanut or vegetable oil
—
2 tbsp (30 ml) lime juice
—
2 tbsp (30 ml)
honey or maple syrup
—
1 garlic clove, minced
—
1/4 tsp (1 ml)
hot pepper flakes or
sambal oelek

* * *

Two 10 1/2 oz (300 g)
pork tenderloins
—
1 lb (500 g)
green beans or asparagus
—
8 oz (225 g) cremini mushrooms
—
8 oz (225 g) oyster mushrooms,
cut into large pieces
—
4 garlic cloves, crushed
—
1/4 cup (60 ml) olive oil
—
Salt and freshly ground pepper
—
1 cup (250 ml) chicken stock
—
1/2 cup (125 ml) flat-leaf parsley,
chives or diced tomatoes

* * *

In a resealable plastic bag, place soy sauce, peanut oil, lime juice, honey, garlic and hot pepper flakes and mix well. Add pork, coat well with marinade and reseal bag.
—
Marinate in refrigerator for 30 minutes or more.
—
Preheat oven to 400°F (200°C).
—
Remove pork from marinade, reserving marinade.
—
In a large pan, sear meat on all sides over high heat, approximately 4 minutes. Keep warm.
—
On a large oiled baking sheet, place beans, mushrooms and garlic. Avoid piling vegetables on top of each other.
—
Drizzle vegetables with olive oil and season to taste with salt and pepper. Stir to coat.
—
Place pork on top of vegetables.
—
Cook, uncovered, for 15 to 20 minutes or until internal temperature reaches 145 to 150°F (63 to 65°C) on an instant-read thermometer. Let rest on counter for 10 minutes, covered.
—
Meanwhile, pour marinade and chicken stock into a small saucepan and bring to a boil. Simmer for 5 minutes.

* * *

*Serve
Garnished with parsley, chives or diced tomatoes and topped with sauce.*

*Variation
For carb lovers, add 8 baby potatoes, cut in half and cooked in boiling salted water, to the vegetables on the baking sheet.*

Italian Sausages with Grapes

I love spontaneity!
Cooking with natural gas suits me because it reacts quickly. The flame fuses the aromas,
sears the food and caramelizes on command—improving my food.

Serves 4

* * *

1 1/3 lbs (670 g)
Italian sausages

—

2 tbsp (30 ml)
olive oil

—

3 cups (750 ml) sweet red
seedless grapes or, if in season,
seedless Muscat grapes

—

Salt and freshly ground pepper

—

Olive oil (optional)

* * *

Prick sausages all over with a fork.
Place in a pot filled with hot water,
bring to a boil and blanch for
5 minutes.

—

Remove sausages from water and
pat dry.

—

Slice each sausage into two or
three pieces.

—

In a large frying pan, heat oil
and brown sausages for 5 to
8 minutes, turning often.

—

Reserve 2 tbsp (30 ml) cooking fat
in frying pan or remove cooking
fat and replace with 2 tbsp (30 ml) of
olive oil.

Add grapes to pan.

—

Cook over medium heat, partially
covered, stirring frequently, for
5 to 10 minutes.

* * *

Serve
With Polenta (p. 129),
green beans, rapini or flavoured
Mashed Potatoes (p. 122)

Note
If the grapes give off too much juice,
remove them with a slotted spoon
along with the sausages. Reduce juice
over high heat until syrupy. Return
grapes and sausages to sauce.

Sausages with Figs

A delicious marriage of sausage and fruit from chef Franca Mezza
that celebrates the all-too-short fig season.

Serves 4

* * *

4 mild or hot Italian
sausages or chorizo sausages

—

Olive oil

—

8 fresh or dried figs

—

Fresh fine herbs
(thyme, basil or sage)

* * *

In a frying pan, brown sausages in oil.

—

Cut four slits in each sausage.

—

Continue cooking until no longer pink
in centre.

—

Reduce heat and place figs among
sausages. Sprinkle with selected
herbs.

Cook just long enough to heat figs,
shaking pan.

—

Slice sausages thickly. Place with figs
and herbs on heated serving platter.

* * *

Champvallon

Our visit to chef Martin Picard led us to discover champvallon,
a French classic made with onions, cubed meat and potatoes.
A unique, festive dish, ideal for entertaining.

Serves 6 to 8

* * *

2 1/3 lbs (1.2 kg)
game, lamb or
pork shoulder, cubed

—

Plenty of olive oil or butter

—

Salt and freshly ground pepper

—

Plenty of chicken stock

—

6 large onions, sliced

—

6 yellow potatoes,
peeled and sliced

—

3 tbsp (45 ml)
chopped garlic, or to taste

—

Fresh thyme to taste or
2 tsp (10 ml) dried thyme

—

Butter
(optional)

* * *

In a large frying pan, sear meat in oil until well browned. Season with salt and pepper while cooking. Set aside.

—

Remove cooking fat and deglaze pan with stock, scraping brown bits from bottom. Set aside with browned meat.

—

In the same pan, melt butter over low heat and gently caramelize onions for 15 to 20 minutes, stirring frequently, until golden brown. Set aside separately.

—

Preheat over to 400°F (200°C).

—

In a large baking dish, lay out half of the potato slices in a pinwheel pattern. Season with salt. Top with half of the onions. Add half each of the garlic and thyme.

Spread all of the meat with its juices over top and season with remaining garlic and thyme. Cover completely with remaining onions and repeat seasoning to taste.

Top with remaining potatoes in pinwheel pattern. Season with salt.

—

Press the champvallon down to submerge it in the stock. Add more stock as needed to cover. Top with a few dollops of butter, if desired.

Cover with aluminum foil. Place dish on a rimmed baking sheet before putting it in the oven.

—

Bake 30 minutes. Reduce heat to 325°F (160°C).

—

Bake, covered, for 2 hours or until meat is tender.

—

Uncover for the last 30 minutes of cooking.

—

Brown at 450°F (230°C), if needed.

* * *

Serve
As chef Martin Picard does,
with mustard and coarse sea salt

—

With a seasonal green salad and
mustard-laced vinaigrette

Lamb Braised en Papillote

*It's fun to wrap a piece of meat with a few sprigs of herbs
and serve it five hours later, juicy and flavourful. For this, I thank my friends Roger and Françoise.
The first time I tasted this recipe, it was made with a leg of lamb. Here, I use a shoulder,
which is just as tasty and more economical.*

/ 086

Serves 4

* * *

Plenty of olive oil
—
2 tsp (10 ml) salt
—
Freshly ground pepper
—
1 lamb shoulder,
2 lbs (1 kg),
or short leg of lamb,
4 1/4 lbs (2 kg)
—
8 cloves garlic, unpeeled
—
4 large sprigs rosemary

* * *

Preheat oven to 250°F (120°C).
—
Lay two or three 2-ft (60 cm) sheets of parchment paper or aluminum foil in a cross pattern in a broiling pan.
—
Rub oil, salt and freshly ground pepper onto lamb.
—
Place garlic and half of the rosemary on parchment and top with meat.
—
Add remaining rosemary.
—
Wrap paper around meat to make a sealed package. Add a third sheet if needed, as it is important that the package be completely sealed to hold in juices.
—
Bake for 5 hours.
—
Open package and remove juices.
—
Cut meat with a spoon, without attempting to slice it, and serve with cooking juices (jus) and one garlic clove per person, for crushing into the jus.

* * *

*Serve
With Lentil Stew (p. 126)
—
With blanched green beans
reheated in a little olive oil
—
With Mashed Potatoes
with peas or lemon (p. 122) or
Sweet Potato Mash (p. 123)*

Lamb Hash

* * *

Why not take advantage of this opportunity to cook two pieces of meat? You can use the rest to make a delicious hash.

* * *

In a frying pan, sauté a thinly sliced onion in a little butter or olive oil until translucent.
—
Transfer onion to a generously buttered baking dish and top with cubed cooked lamb.
—
Crush garlic cloves into cooking juices and pour over meat.
—
Season to taste.
—
Top with lemon-scented Mashed Potatoes or Mashed Potatoes with Peas (p. 122), Sweet Potato Mash with Olives (p. 123) or Mashed Celeriac (p. 123).
—
Bake at 350°F (180°C) for 30 minutes.

* * *

*Serve
With ketchup, chutney or
a green salad*

Braised Beef with Star Anise

The pleasure of a braised dish, a simple preparation flavoured with star anise.
If you can find short ribs, try this version, as the bone gives the dish a special flavour.

/ 089

Serves 6 to 8

* * *

4 lbs (1.6 kg)
blade or cross rib roast
or 5 to 6 lbs (2.25 to 2.75 kg)
trimmed short ribs

—

Salt and freshly ground pepper

—

3 tbsp (45 ml)
vegetable oil

—

3 yellow onions,
quartered, or
2 bunches green onions, sliced

—

6 carrots, cut in large chunks

—

4 garlic cloves, crushed

—

3 cups (750 ml)
beef stock

—

1/3 cup (80 ml)
soy sauce or tamari

—

2 tbsp (30 ml)
tomato paste

—

1 to 2 tbsp (15 to 30 ml)
brown sugar

—

1 piece (2 in / 5 cm)
fresh ginger, sliced

—

4 star anise

* * *

Preheat oven to 325°F (160°C).

—

Season meat generously with
salt and pepper.

—

In a large casserole, brown meat on
all sides over medium-high heat
in 2 tbsp (30 ml) of the oil. Set aside.

—

Discard cooking fat. In same pan,
brown onions and carrots over
medium heat for 5 minutes in
remaining oil.

—

Add garlic and cook for 1 minute.

—

Place meat on vegetables. Add stock,
soy sauce, tomato paste, brown sugar,
ginger and star anise.

—

Bring to a boil, then bake in oven,
covered, for at least 3 hours or until
meat falls off the bone.

—

After 1 hour of cooking, turn meat
pieces and check that liquid is at least
halfway up meat. Check liquid level
again 1 hour later, adding additional
water or stock if necessary.

When meat is cooked, remove it
from gravy and keep warm.

—

Skim fat from gravy and strain, if
desired, pressing down on vegetables
to extract as much of their juices
as possible.

—

Return meat to gravy. Cut meat with
serving spoon, without attempting to
slice it.

* * *

Serve
With Mashed Potatoes of
your choice (p. 122)

—

With Bok Choy (p. 114)

—

Or with a green vegetable (p. 114)

Osso Bucco with Fennel and Gremolata

This dish is so good reheated!

Serves 6

* * *

6 veal shanks,
1 1/2 in (4 cm) thick
(3 lbs / 1.5 kg)

—

Salt and freshly ground pepper

—

Flour (optional)

—

Olive oil

—

2 fennel bulbs,
trimmed (p. 173) and quartered

—

1 cup (250 ml)
orange juice

—

2 long ribbons orange zest

—

1 cup (250 ml)
chicken or veal stock

—

1 can (14 oz / 398 ml)
diced tomatoes

—

1 bay leaf

—

1 tsp (5 ml)
crushed fennel seeds

* * *

Preheat oven to 375°F (190°C).

—

Season meat with salt and pepper,
and flour, if desired.

—

In a large pot, heat oil over
medium-high heat.

—

Sear meat on all sides, approximately
2 minutes per side. Set aside.

—

Sauté fennel in a little oil until
slightly browned. Set aside.

—

Reduce heat. Deglaze pot with
orange juice, scraping brown bits
from bottom.

—

Return meat to pot and add zest,
stock, tomatoes, bay leaf, fennel
seeds and salt and pepper to taste.

—

Bake, covered, for 45 minutes.

—

Turn shanks, add fennel and cover.

—

Cook for 45 minutes to 1 hour more
until meat is tender and falling off
the bone.

* * *

Serve

*With pasta with butter or oil.
Coat with Gremolata (below)*

—

*With Mashed Potatoes with
Saffron or other mash (p. 122)*

—

Or with Polenta (p. 129)

Variation

*Carrots may be added at the
same time as the fennel.*

Gremolata

* * *

Flat-leaf parsley,
finely chopped

—

Lemon or orange zest, or both

—

Garlic, minced (optional)

* * *

Mix parsley, zest and garlic (if using).
Sprinkle over each portion before
serving.

—

Sprinkle as a garnish over mashed
potatoes, pasta, rice or braised
dishes. Gremolata may be prepared
ahead of time and kept in the
refrigerator for a few hours.

* * *

— Pastas, Pizzas —
and Grilled Sandwiches

* * *

Tomato sauce

Tomato sauce is essential! Here is a basic recipe you can adapt to any occasion.
Here I offer two serving suggestions—one with a Parmesan coulis, the other flavoured with mint.
Let your inspiration guide you.

Makes enough
for 1 lb (500 g) of pasta
* * *
3 tbsp (45 ml)
olive oil or butter
—
1 or 2 garlic cloves, peeled,
germ removed and chopped
—
1 can (28 oz / 796 ml)
tomatoes, diced or whole,
chopped in food processor
—
Salt
—
Sugar (optional)
—
1/2 cup (125 ml)
fresh basil, chopped
—
1/4 cup (60 ml)
flat-leaf parsley, chopped
* * *

<u>In a large saucepan</u>, heat oil.
—
<u>Fry</u> garlic over low heat, taking care
not to let it colour.
—
<u>Add</u> tomatoes, salt, sugar (if using),
half the basil and parsley.
—
<u>Adjust</u> seasoning.
—
<u>Simmer</u>, partially covered, for
20 minutes or until sauce reaches
desired consistency.
—
<u>Add</u> remaining basil at the end
of cooking.
* * *

Serve
With grated Romano, Parmesan
or ricotta salata cheese
—
With Parmesan Coulis (below)

Store
Store containers of tomato sauce
in the freezer. Allow a few extra
minutes when reheating for the
water accumulated through freezing
to evaporate.

Mint-Tomato Sauce

* * *

<u>Make</u> the sauce with butter
instead of olive oil. Replace the
basil with 1/4 cup (60 ml) chopped
fresh mint, added 5 minutes before
end of cooking time.
* * *

Parmesan Coulis

Yield: 2/3 cup (160 ml)
* * *
1/2 cup (125 ml)
low-sodium chicken stock
—
1/2 cup (125 ml) 35% cream
—
1/2 cup (125 ml)
grated Parmesan cheese
* * *

<u>In a saucepan</u> over high heat,
reduce stock by half.
—
<u>Add</u> cream and reduce by a third,
approximately 3 minutes.
—
<u>Add</u> cheese and whisk until
thoroughly blended.
* * *

Serve
As a coulis with Tomato Sauce.
This sauce combination is perfect
with stuffed pasta.

Pasta Pepe e Cacio

*A Roman pasta dish of stunning simplicity
— just noodles with pepper and cheese —
that can rest on its laurels!*

Serves 4

★ ★ ★

1 lb (500 g) pasta

—

2 to 4 tbsp (30 to 60 ml)
butter or olive oil
or equal parts of each

—

2 tsp (10 ml)
coarsely ground pepper

—

1 1/3 cups (330 ml)
grated Romano
or Parmesan cheese
or equal parts of each

—

Grated lemon zest and
lemon juice (optional)

★ ★ ★

<u>In a large pot</u>, cook pasta
in boiling salted water according
to package directions.

<u>Meanwhile</u>, place butter with
pepper on a hot serving platter.
You may place this platter on the
pasta cooking pot to keep it hot.

—

<u>Drain</u> pasta, reserving 1 cup
(250 ml) of the cooking liquid.

—

<u>Transfer</u> pasta to platter and
toss to coat with peppery butter.

—

<u>Add</u> 1 cup (250 ml) of the cheese,
a little at a time, stirring and adding
a little cooking liquid as needed.

—

<u>Add</u> remaining cheese, and lemon
zest and juice (if using).

★ ★ ★

Pasta Caponata

Caponata, or pasta with eggplant, may be served warm or cold. The possibilities are endless.

Serves 4

* * *

1 or 2 medium eggplants
(500 to 750 g / 1 to 1 1/2 lbs),
with skin, cubed

—

2 stalks celery, cubed

—

1 large onion,
coarsely chopped

—

2 red bell peppers, cubed

—

Olive oil

—

1/4 cup (60 ml)
wine vinegar

—

1 tbsp (15 ml) sugar

—

6 plum tomatoes,
seeded but unpeeled, or
1 can (14 oz / 398 ml)
plum tomatoes,
well drained

—

1/3 to 1/2 cup (80 to 125 ml)
green or black olives,
pitted and chopped

—

Salt and freshly ground pepper

—

1/4 tsp (1 ml)
hot pepper flakes or
sambal oelek

—

Capers, to taste (optional)

—

Penne or other short pasta,
cooked, drained and unrinsed

* * *

Preheat oven to 400°F (200°C).

—

Line one large or two medium rimmed
baking sheets with parchment paper
or aluminum foil.

—

Combine eggplant, celery, onion
and bell pepper and generously coat
with oil.

—

Add vinegar, sugar, tomatoes and
olives. Mix well.

—

Season with salt, pepper and
hot pepper flakes.

—

Spread vegetables over baking
sheet(s). If using a single baking
sheet, place it in the centre of the
oven. If using two, place one in the
centre and the other on the lower
rack, then alternate every 15 minutes,
slightly increasing cooking time,
if needed.

—

Roast vegetables for 50 minutes,
stirring twice. Remove from oven.

—

If using fresh tomatoes, remove skins.

—

Transfer vegetables to a bowl.

—

Add capers (if using).

* * *

Variation

*For a light meal, serve Caponata with
poached eggs or use it to fill an
omelette before folding.*

—

*As a main dish, serve Caponata
on toast or with tuna.*

Note

*Prepare caponata ahead
of time to let flavours blend.*

Serve

Over pasta with a drizzle of oil

—

Alongside grilled fish or chicken

Sausage and Spinach Pasta

A rustic, tasty and satisfying pasta dish.

Serves 4

* * *

Olive oil

—

1 large Spanish onion,
cut in half then sliced

—

1 lb (500 g)
mild or hot Italian sausages, or
equal parts of each, casings
removed, crumbled

—

Approximately 1 1/2 cups
(375 ml) chicken stock

—

1 lb (500 g)
penne, orecchiette or
fusilli pasta

—

4 cups (1 l)
spinach* or baby spinach

—

Salt and freshly ground pepper

—

4 tbsp (60 ml)
grated Parmesan or
pecorino cheese, or to taste

* * *

In a large frying pan, gently
heat oil. Add onion and brown
slightly, stirring.

—

Add sausage meat and cook,
breaking up, until no longer pink.

—

Pour in 1 cup (250 ml) of the stock
and reduce for a few minutes to
blend flavours.

—

In a large pot of boiling salted water,
cook pasta according to package
directions.

—

Drain pasta without rinsing.
Add to sauce along with spinach.
Season with salt and pepper and mix
well. Reheat with remaining stock,
shaking the pan.

—

Stir in cheese.

* * *

Variation
The spinach may be replaced with
trimmed blanched rapini,
drained and coarsely chopped.

*If using spinach leaves, rinse them and remove
ribs. Chop coarsely and place in a large strainer.
Pour pasta cooking liquid over spinach and drain.

Pizza Dough

*A recipe by my friend Elena Faita that Stephano, her son,
made with gusto on our show!*

*Makes four 16-in (41 cm) pizzas or
two 15- x 20-in (38 x 50 cm) pizzas*

* * *

50 g fresh cake yeast
or 2 tbsp (30 ml)
dry yeast

—

1 tbsp (15 ml) sugar

—

2 1/2 cups (625 ml)
warm water (38°C / 100°F)

—

4 cups (1 l) OO* or
all-purpose flour

—

2 cups (500 ml)
wheat semolina

—

1 tbsp (15 ml) salt

* * *

*Elena and Stephano prefer this high-gluten flour
because it is finer, but this recipe works just as
well using all-purpose flour.

In a bowl, mix yeast, sugar and hot water. Stir to dissolve completely. If using dry yeast, let stand for 10 minutes.

—

In a large bowl, sift together flour, semolina and salt.

—

Pour yeast mixture over dry ingredients and mix.

—

Knead until dough becomes elastic, 5 to 8 minutes. Add more flour as needed.

—

Divide dough in half and place in two separate oiled bowls.

—

Cover dough with a clean towel and let rise for 45 minutes or until doubled in volume. A handy warm place to let dough rise is an unheated oven with the light on.

—

Punch down dough and knead it again for several minutes.

—

Put dough back into bowls, cover and let rise again for 45 minutes or until doubled in volume.

—

Roll out dough and spread on generously oiled baking sheet. Let rise for 5 to 10 minutes.

—

Preheat oven to 425°F (220°C).

Top with tomato sauce, such as Quick Tomato Sauce (p. 104), toppings and selected cheeses and bake for 15 to 30 minutes until crust is golden brown and cheese is melted.

* * *

Focaccia

*Serve as an hors d'oeuvre,
a side dish or a sandwich.*

* * *

Divide dough into four pieces and roll out each one with a rolling pin into a rough 10-in (25 cm) shape (round, oval or square).

—

Place dough on a baking sheet. Prick all over with a fork, cover with a damp towel and let rise for about 1 hour, until doubled in volume.

—

Preheat oven to 425°F (220°C).

—

Brush dough generously with olive oil.

—

Sprinkle with coarse salt or fleur de sel and chopped rosemary.

—

Bake for 20 to 30 minutes, until crust is golden.

* * *

Egg Pizza

The idea here was to present you with a tomato-and-cheese-based pizza.
Look no further, you've found it! This raw tomato sauce by Gilbert Sicotte is perfect for pizza.
As for toppings, have fun with them! This pizza is topped with eggs.

Serves 4

* * *

Pizza
—

1 lb (500 g)
commercial pizza dough
or see recipe (p. 103)

Quick Tomato Sauce
—

1 can (14 oz / 398 ml)
plum tomatoes,
diced or whole,
coarsely chopped
—
2 tbsp (30 ml)
olive oil
—
Salt and freshly ground pepper
—
Fresh basil, chopped,
and/or dried oregano
—
1 garlic clove, chopped
—
2 tbsp (30 ml)
Parmesan cheese

* * *

Toppings
—

2 cups (500 ml)
mozzarella cheese,
7 oz (200 g)
—
3 tbsp (45 ml)
olive oil
—
4 eggs
—
Salt and freshly ground pepper

* * *

If using frozen pizza dough, oil it and place it in a bowl. Cover with a damp towel and thaw in refrigerator overnight or on the counter for 6 hours.

—

Preheat oven to 425°F (220°C).

—

Divide dough into four equal parts.

—

Roll out each part into an 8-in (20 cm) diameter disk.

—

Let dough rise for 5 minutes.

—

Before preparing sauce, drain tomatoes thoroughly.

—

In a bowl, combine tomatoes, oil, salt and pepper to taste, basil, oregano (if using), garlic and Parmesan.

—

Spread sauce over dough and sprinkle with mozzarella. Drizzle oil over in a zigzag pattern. Place pizzas on baking sheet. Bake for 5 minutes on bottom rack.

—

Remove from oven and push topping aside from centre of each pizza to create a cavity. Break an egg into each. Season to taste with salt and pepper.

—

Return pizzas to oven and cook for another 10 minutes or until pizzas are golden brown and egg yolks are runny.

* * *

Serve
Topped with baby spinach or arugula salad after removing pizza from oven
—
Drizzled with Pepper Oil (p. 176)
—
With a fresh basil chiffonade

Pissaladière

The onion, easy to find and so tasty when gently caramelized.
Try this onion pizza for a quick lunch or with drinks.

Serves 6 to 8

* * *

2 lbs (1 kg) onions or
3 Spanish onions, thinly sliced

—

Olive oil

—

2 large garlic cloves,
finely diced

—

Fresh or dried thyme

—

Salt and freshly ground pepper

—

4 plum tomatoes, peeled,
seeded and diced, or
1 can (14 oz / 398 ml)
diced tomatoes

—

1 lb (500 g)
bread dough or ready-made
frozen pizza dough
or see recipe (p. 103)

* * *

Toppings, to taste

—

Anchovy fillets, drained,
halved lengthwise

—

Red peppers packed in water,
drained, cut into strips

—

Roasted peppers, grilled,
peeled and cut into strips (p. 179)

—

Pitted black olives, halved

* * *

Do this step ahead of time

—

In a large frying pan, sauté onions in
oil over low heat until softened and
cooking juices are released, about
15 minutes. Cook, covered, for
5 minutes.

—

Stir in garlic, thyme, salt and pepper.
Add tomatoes.

—

Continue cooking for another
20 minutes, uncovered, shaking pan
from time to time. The bottom of the
pan should be almost dry.

—

Remove from heat and set aside

* * *

Preheat oven to 450°F (230°C).
Place rack in bottom third of oven.

—

On an oiled baking sheet, spread
dough with hands to form a 10- x
15-in (25 x 38 cm) surface. Cover
dough with waxed paper.

—

Let rise for 15 minutes.

—

Brush edges with oil.

—

Spread onion mixture over dough,
leaving a 1/2-in (1.5 cm) edge.

—

Lay out anchovies or pepper strips
in a diamond pattern. Garnish
with black olives, if desired. Brush
with olive oil.

—

Cook for 25 to 30 minutes or until
crust is golden and crispy.

* * *

Serve
As an appetizer or with raw
vegetables and a glass of rosé
—
As a main dish with a salad

Grilled Cheese

Irresistible at any time of day, impossible to fumble,
crispy outside and melty inside.

Bread

* * *

Have fun trying different
types—multigrain, country-style,
caraway, black olive, nut, etc.

* * *

Fillings, to taste

* * *

_ Italian cheese (provolone, mozzarella, fontina or taleggio) and sautéed mushrooms
_ Italian or goat cheese, with sun-dried tomato pesto or strips, or diced olives
_ Blue cheese, lightened with a milder cheese, with sliced pears on nut bread
_ Cheddar and marinated hot peppers on caraway bread
_ Cheddar with sliced drained tomatoes, and arugula or watercress leaves
_ Swiss cheese, Dijon mustard, cooked bacon or ham, and diced drained tomatoes on country-style bread
_ Classic Oka cheese with sliced apples
_ Leftover fine cheese on nut bread

* * *

* * *

Butter bread or brush oil on one side of each slice. Top unbuttered side with selected filling. Place second slice on top, buttered or oiled side up.

—

Grill in cast-iron, nonstick or ribbed frying pan until bread is golden and cheese begins to melt. Flatten sandwich by laying a small cast-iron pan on top.

* * *

— Sides —

* * *

Zucchini-Tomato Tian

A colourful, sunny dish that can be prepared ahead of time, any time of year.
Magnificent served directly from the oven.

/ 112

Serves 6 to 8

* * *

3 or 4 small onions,
sliced in 3/8-in (1 cm) rounds
—
2 garlic cloves, minced
—
2 tsp (10 ml)
herbes de Provence
—
Salt
—
1/3 cup (80 ml)
olive oil
—
2 yellow zucchinis,
sliced 3/8 in (1 cm) thick
—
2 green zucchinis,
sliced 3/8 in (1 cm) thick
—
4 or 5 Italian tomatoes,
sliced 3/8 in (1 cm) thick
—
Grated Parmesan or
other grated cheese (optional)

* * *

Preheat oven to 400°F (200°C).
—
Line bottom of baking dish with
onions, half of the garlic, half of the
herbes de Provence and salt. Drizzle
with half of the olive oil.
—
Overlap sliced vegetables slightly in
dish, alternating colours. Season with
salt and sprinkle remaining garlic,
herbs and oil evenly over top.
—
Bake for at least 1 hour or until
vegetables are very tender.
—
Sprinkle with Parmesan, if desired,
and continue cooking for another
5 to 10 minutes.

* * *

Serve
For a vegetarian meal,
serve with Polenta (p. 129)

As an appetizer, serve with a hunk of
Parmesan, a bottle of olive oil, and
some good bread and wine.
—
Also delicious at room temperature.

Greens

Must-haves!

Braised Bok Choy

Serves 4

* * *

1 lb (500 g) small bok choy
or Shanghai choy, washed
in plenty of water

—

2 tbsp (30 ml) butter or oil

—

Green onions, sliced to taste

—

Salt

—

1/2 cup (125 ml)
chicken stock or water

* * *

If the bok choy are a little large,
cut them in half or in quarters
lengthwise.

—

In a large frying pan, heat butter and
add bok choy, green onions and salt.

—

Cook over high heat until bok choy
begins to colour. Moisten with stock
or water, cover and cook vegetables
until tender-crisp.

* * *

Steamed Bok Choy

* * *

If the bok choy are a little large,
cut them lengthwise, steam for
a few minutes and sprinkle with
a little vinaigrette.

Or reheat bok choy in oil with
minced green onion and a dash of
soy sauce or tamari.

Bok choy may be seasoned with a
spoonful of oyster sauce.

You can also reheat bok choy in
the cooking juices from a roast or
other meat.

* * *

Spinach

Serves 4

* * *

2 tbsp (30 ml)
olive oil

—

1 garlic clove,
cut in half (optional)

—

20 oz (600 g)
fresh spinach,
trimmed, rinsed, drained

—

Salt

—

Lemon wedges or
grated nutmeg, to taste

* * *

In a large pan, heat oil over
medium heat. If you are using garlic,
brown it lightly. Add spinach and
cook quickly, turning or stirring until
the leaves wilt. Season with salt.

—

Serve with a lemon wedge or
grated nutmeg.

* * *

Broccoli

Serves 4

* * *

1 1/2 lb (750 g) broccoli

* * *

Seasoning

—

Olive oil

—

1 lemon quarter or
Lemon Oil (p. 176)

—

Salt and freshly ground pepper

* * *

<u>Cut</u> broccoli into florets.
Peel stem and slice lengthwise.

—

<u>In a pan filled with boiling salted water</u>, cook broccoli or steam in a vegetable steamer.

<u>Drain</u> broccoli while still crisp and add a dash of olive oil to taste and a lemon quarter (or simply substitute lemon oil). Season with salt and pepper to taste.

* * *

Rapini

Loved by some, hated by others, rapini's bitterness leaves no one indifferent. It is an underappreciated vegetable! When buying rapini, avoid yellow buds and woody stems.

* * *

Serves 4

* * *

1 bunch rapini
(1 1/3 lb / 600 g)

—

Olive oil

—

Garlic, minced (optional)

—

Salt

* * *

<u>Trim</u> approximately 1/2 in (1.5 cm) or more off stems and remove any wilted leaves, reserving the rest. Separate stems into two parts: 4-in (10 cm) florets and the rest of the stem.

—

<u>In a pan filled with salted boiling water</u>, blanch stems for approximately 30 seconds. Add florets and blanch for a few seconds more.

—

<u>Chill</u> in ice water to stop cooking. Partially drain.

—

<u>In a frying pan</u>, heat oil. Fry garlic, if desired, without browning. Add wet rapini. Season with salt.

—

<u>Cover</u> and continue cooking over medium heat until tender-crisp. Serve.

* * *

Roasted Vegetables

So good!
The flavour is more concentrated and the vegetables are lightly caramelized.
These are delicious as a side dish, but also as an entrée and in a salad.
Don't forget to add them to pasta dishes, too.

Basic Principles

*   *   *

Use a large baking sheet with a low rim (less than 2 in/5 cm). The vegetables must not touch one another, so that they roast rather than steam.

—

Oil the baking sheet or lining paper (line baking sheet with parchment paper or aluminum foil for easy clean-up).

—

Cut vegetables into even pieces for uniform cooking. Thoroughly coat vegetables with oil in a bag or bowl. Season to taste.

—

Use coarse sea salt if you have it and coarsely chopped herbs for seasoning (rosemary, thyme or sage). Or experiment with spices.

*Never store garlic in oil at room temperature. Always refrigerate it, and keep it for no more than one week to prevent dangerous bacteria from growing.

Preheat oven to 425°F (220°C), unless otherwise noted.

—

If you are using a single baking sheet, place it in centre of oven. If you must use two baking sheets, place one in the centre and the other on the lower rack, alternating every 15 minutes and increasing cooking time slightly.

—

While cooking, occasionally shake baking sheet or turn vegetables with a spatula or tongs to roast evenly. **Cooking times are approximate and depend on the baking sheet as well as the quantity and freshness of the vegetables.**

*   *   *

Roasted Garlic

A nutty flavour, milder and more easily digested than raw garlic. Dividing the head of garlic into cloves makes extracting the roasted garlic much easier. It handily replaces raw garlic in all kinds of preparations: mayonnaise, salad dressings, pesto or sauce.

*   *   *

1 or 2 heads garlic,
divided into cloves, unpeeled

—

Olive oil

*   *   *

Preheat oven to 350°F (180°C).

—

Place cloves in centre of a square of aluminum foil.

—

Add a generous dollop of oil and wrap in foil. Bake in centre of oven for 45 minutes.

—

Now you just need to press the clove to extract the roasted garlic. Purée if desired.

—

Keeps in refrigerator for a few days, or in a tightly closed container, covered in oil*.

*   *   *

Serve
Spread on bread

—

Add to salad dressing or mayonnaise (p. 178)

—

Blend into a vegetable purée

—

Add to sauces, soups, pesto, etc.

Asparagus
* * *

(To trim asparagus, see p. 170.)
Oil, salt and roast asparagus for
10 to 15 minutes. Shake baking sheet
halfway through cooking time.
Prick asparagus to test for doneness.

* * *

Beets
* * *

Wrap unpeeled, oiled beets in
foil. Roast for about 45 minutes,
depending on season and size of
beets. Prick with tip of knife to test
for doneness.

* * *

Carrots and Parsnip
* * *

Cut in half lengthwise, or leave whole
if vegetables are thin. Oil, salt, stir
and roast for 30 to 40 minutes, turning
halfway through cooking time.

* * *

Cauliflower
* * *

Cut cauliflower into 2-in (5 cm)
florets. Oil, salt, season with curry
powder and roast for about
30 minutes, stirring once or twice.

* * *

Winter, Butternut and Buttercup Squash
* * *

Do not peel. Cut squash into
1 1/2-in (4 cm) wedges. Oil, salt,
season with spices and/or herbs
(cayenne, thyme, coriander seeds
or rosemary) and roast for about
40 minutes, turning twice during
cooking time.

* * *

Fennel
* * *

(To trim fennel, see p. 173.)
Cut fennel into 6 wedges. Add oil
and salt. Roast for about 40 minutes,
turning twice during cooking time.

* * *

Green Beans
* * *

Trim beans, add salt and oil, and roast
for about 10 to 15 minutes, shaking
baking sheet after 5 minutes. Avoid
roasting string beans.

* * *

Onions
* * *

Cut peeled medium-sized onions
into wedges without cutting through
core. Add oil and salt and roast for
15 minutes. Turn and cook for another
15 minutes.

—

Peel, oil and salt small whole cipollini
onions and cook for 20 to 30 minutes.

* * *

Sweet Potatoes
* * *

Peel and cut potatoes into wedges.
Add oil, salt and seasoning to taste
(allspice, cumin, rosemary or garlic).
Roast for about 40 minutes, turning
twice during cooking time.

* * *

Potatoes
* * *

Cut into wedges. Add oil and salt and
roast for about 40 minutes, turning
twice during cooking time.

* * *

Cherry Tomatoes
* * *

Place oiled tomatoes on baking
sheet. Roast for 10 minutes at 450°F
(230°C) or until tender. Add salt and
freshly ground pepper.

—

Serve hot or at room temperature.

* * *

Pepperonata

One of my mother's recipes—which she often cooks without tomatoes—is so delicious with so many things that she always has some in her fridge or freezer. She adds a spoonful of these stewed peppers and tomatoes to all kinds of dishes, whether main courses or sides.

Serves 6

* * *

5 red, yellow or orange bell peppers, grilled and peeled (p. 179)

—

1/3 cup (80 ml) olive oil

—

2 garlic cloves, peeled, germ removed and diced

—

1 bay leaf

—

1 can (14 oz / 398 ml) Italian tomatoes, drained, or 5 plum tomatoes, peeled and seeded

—

Salt and freshly ground pepper

* * *

Cut peppers into wedges.

—

Heat oil in a large frying pan over medium-high heat. Fry peppers for 5 minutes, stirring often, to caramelize lightly. Add salt.

Add garlic, bay leaf and tomatoes. Crush tomatoes with a wooden spoon. Simmer over medium-low heat for 10 to 15 minutes or until stewed. Check from time to time to prevent vegetables from sticking.

—

Adjust seasoning and serve warm.

* * *

Serve

On a slice of toasted country-style bread rubbed with garlic

—

With a few slices of mozzarella or a few shards of Parmesan and good crusty bread

—

Alongside roasted or grilled meats (steak, sausages or chicken)

—

As a sauce over pasta

—

As a garnish for eggs

Variation

Add a small hot pepper if you like.

Mashed Potatoes

Mashed potatoes are an all-time favourite, whether whipped or chunky, simple or sophisticated!

Serves 4 to 6

* * *

2 lb (1 kg) potatoes
(Yukon, Idaho or Charlotte),
peeled and quartered

—

Salt

—

Butter

—

Cream or milk

—

Freshly ground pepper

—

Grated nutmeg

* * *

In a saucepan, cover potatoes with generously salted cold water. Bring to a boil and lower heat. Simmer, covered, for 15 to 20 minutes.

—

Drain and return potatoes to pan; place pan on burner to dry potatoes well. Mash potatoes with ricer or masher. Blend in butter, cream, pepper and nutmeg to taste. Adjust seasoning.

* * *

With Olive Oil

* * *

Replace cream or milk and butter with olive oil. If desired, add diced pitted olives. With olives, omit nutmeg.

* * *

With Mustard

* * *

Omit nutmeg. Once mash is ready, add approximately 2 tbsp (30 ml) Dijon or old-fashioned mustard. Delicious with sausages, roasts, lamb, chicken and fish.

* * *

With Garlic Purée

* * *

Add 4 cloves roasted garlic (p. 117) just before mashing.

* * *

With Arugula

* * *

Chop a large bunch of arugula into a chiffonade and add to mashed potatoes with olive oil, using roasted garlic if desired.

* * *

With Lemon

* * *

Before mashing potatoes, melt butter and add 2 tsp (10 ml) finely grated lemon zest and 2 tsp (10 ml) lemon juice. Once mashed, garnish with chopped parsley or gremolata (p. 90.)

* * *

With Saffron

* * *

For saffron lovers—add a whole onion, quartered, when cooking potatoes. Infuse two pinches of saffron in heated milk or cream for 15 minutes. Continue basic recipe, omitting nutmeg. This recipe produces a mash of a beautiful yellow colour that marries wonderfully with Osso Bucco (p. 90) or fish.

* * *

With Peas

* * *

Cook potatoes with an onion. Around 5 to 10 minutes before potatoes are cooked, add 2 cups (500 ml) frozen peas, thawed. Drain and press through ricer or mash with masher; add butter, cream, salt, pepper and 2 tbsp (30 ml) chopped mint. This mash has a chunky texture.

* * *

With Leeks

* * *

In a frying pan, gently cook sliced leeks in butter and olive oil until soft. Arrange on top of mash.

* * *

Sweet Potato Mash

*Adds colour and flavour.
A wonderful recipe from
Philippe de Vienne's team.*

Serves 4

* * *

2 lb (1 kg) sweet potatoes
(around 3), cut into pieces

—

Plenty of olive oil

—

1 tbsp (15 ml) finely
chopped rosemary

—

Generous pinch grated nutmeg

—

Salt and freshly ground pepper

—

1/3 cup (80 ml)
pitted black olives, quartered

* * *

<u>In a saucepan</u>, steam potatoes,
about 15 minutes. (Potatoes may also
be baked and peeled.)

—

<u>Coarsely</u> mash potato flesh with
a whisk or masher.

<u>Add</u> oil, rosemary, nutmeg, salt and
pepper. Stir in olives.

*Serve
Garnish with black olives,
if desired*

Celeriac Mash

Despite its appearance, celeriac is a fine vegetable with a delicate flavour.

Serves 4

* * *

1 large celeriac bulb,
approximately 2 lb (1 kg),
peeled and cubed

—

1 large potato,
approximately 7 oz (200 g),
peeled and cubed smaller
than the celeriac

—

Plenty of butter, cream or milk

—

Salt and freshly ground pepper

* * *

<u>In a saucepan</u>, cook celeriac and
potato in salted boiling water for
15 to 20 minutes.

—

<u>Drain</u> vegetables and dry them over
the heat, shaking pan.

<u>With a masher</u>, mash vegetables.
With electric mixer, purée finely,
blending in butter. Add salt and
freshly ground pepper.

* * *

Warm Potato Salad with Mustard

The bright green of watercress or arugula,
the sweetness of potato and the tang of mustard.

Serves 4

* * *

1 1/3 lb (670 g) fingerling
or baby potatoes

—

1 tsp (5 ml)
grated lemon zest

—

1 tbsp (15 ml)
lemon juice

—

1 tbsp (15 ml)
old-fashioned mustard

—

Salt and freshly ground pepper

—

1/4 cup (60 ml)
olive oil

—

Bunch chives, dill or
green onions, chopped

—

Sliced radishes or
fennel (optional)

—

Bunch watercress or arugula,
washed and trimmed

* * *

In a saucepan, cover potatoes with generously salted cold water.

—

Bring to a boil and cook potatoes, covered, until tender.

—

Drain and cut potatoes in half, and arrange in a bowl.

—

In a small bowl, whisk lemon zest and juice, mustard, salt, pepper and olive oil.

—

Pour over hot potatoes.

—

Add selected herb and stir to combine.

—

Garnish with radishes or fennel, if desired.

—

Arrange salad on a bed of watercress or lightly oiled arugula or a seasonal green salad.

* * *

Serve

With grilled beef,
chicken or sausages

—

With charcuterie

—

Alongside Salmon Patties (p. 60)

Lentil Stew

*This fabulous stew comes from chef
Josée Robitaille.*

Serves 4

* * *

2 cups (500 ml)
Puy lentils, sorted
—
2 tbsp (30 ml)
duck fat or olive oil
—
1 large onion,
finely chopped
—
2 carrots, diced
—
2 stalks celery, diced
—
1 garlic clove,
peeled and halved
—
4 oz (120 g)
pancetta or
salt pork, diced
—
4 cups (1 l)
vegetable or chicken stock
—
2 sprigs fresh thyme or
1 tsp (5 ml) dried thyme
—
2 bay leaves
—
1 pinch dried savory
—
1/2 cup (125 ml)
flat-leaf parsley, chopped
—
Salt and freshly ground pepper

* * *

<u>Place</u> lentils in pan filled with
water and bring to a boil. Drain
immediately and rinse. Set aside.
—
<u>In a saucepan</u>, melt duck
fat or heat oil over medium heat.
Sweat onion, carrots and celery over
low heat for 10 minutes without
browning them, stirring regularly.
—
<u>Add</u> garlic and pancetta and
continue cooking for 2 minutes.
—
<u>Add</u> stock, thyme, bay leaves,
savory and lentils to vegetables.
—
<u>Reduce</u> heat and cook, covered, for
30 minutes or until tender.
—
<u>Add</u> parsley to lentils, season to
taste with salt and pepper and mix
thoroughly.

* * *

Sides
Great alongside meat confit.

Variation
*To make a soup: add more stock
at cooking time.*

Store
*Can be prepared ahead
of time.*
—
Freezes well.
—
Reheats easily.

Basmati Rice

Basmati rice fills the house with its fragrance as it cooks.
For this method, use a small pan with a tight-fitting lid.

Serves 4

* * *

1 cup (250 ml)
basmati rice*
—
1 tbsp (15 ml)
butter or oil
—
1 1/2 cups (375 ml)
water
—
1/2 tsp (4 ml)
salt

* * *

<u>In a sieve</u>, rinse rice until water runs clear. Drain well, shaking sieve for a few minutes.

—

<u>In a large saucepan</u>, heat butter. Stir-fry rice until well coated. Add water and salt and bring to a boil. Reduce heat to lowest setting.

—

<u>Cook</u>, covered, for about 17 minutes, checking only at end of cooking time. Remove from heat without uncovering. Let rest for 5 to 10 minutes before serving.

* * *

*For 2 cups (500 ml) basmati rice, use 2 3/4 cups (680 ml) water. For 3 cups (750 ml) basmati rice, use 3 3/4 cups (930 ml) water.

Mustard Rice

* * *

<u>Heat</u> mustard seeds in frying pan until they begin to pop. Sprinkle over rice with a few drops of lemon or lime juice before serving.

* * *

Sesame Rice

* * *

<u>Just before serving</u>, add toasted sesame seeds.

* * *

Spiced Rice

* * *

<u>In oil or butter</u>, fry 1 bay leaf, 5 crushed cardamom pods and one 3-in (8 cm) stick cinnamon. Add rice and continue with recipe.

* * *

Brown Basmati Rice

* * *

1 cup (250 ml)
brown basmati rice
—
1 tbsp (15 ml)
oil or butter
—
2 1/4 cups (560 ml)
water
—
1/2 tsp (4 ml)
salt

* * *

<u>Follow</u> recipe for Basmati Rice, increasing cooking time to 40 minutes.

* * *

Baked Polenta

A somewhat non-traditional "baked" version,
but oh so easy.

Serves 4

* * *

3 cups (750 ml) stock

—

1 tbsp (15 ml) butter

—

3/4 cup (180 ml) cornmeal

—

1 tsp (5 ml) salt

—

Freshly ground pepper

—

1/4 cup (60 ml)
grated Parmesan or
cubed Fontina cheese

—

1/4 cup (60 ml)
milk or mascarpone cheese

* * *

<u>Preheat</u> oven to 425°F (220°C).

—

<u>In a roasting pan</u> or saucepan,
mix stock, butter, cornmeal, salt
and pepper.

—

<u>Bake</u>, covered, for 30 minutes, stirring
once halfway through cooking time.

—

<u>Remove</u> from oven; add cheese
and milk.

—

<u>Stir</u> and season to taste.

* * *

Serve
With braised meats
—
Alongside sausages
—
As a vegetarian meal,
with Zucchini-Tomato Tian (p. 112)
and Pepperonata (p. 120)
—
With mushroom stew
—
Simply covered
with Tomato Sauce (p. 94)

Store
In refrigerator. To use up
cold leftover polenta, slice and fry
in oil in a nonstick frying pan.

— Desserts —

* * *

Panna Cotta

Literally, "cooked cream."
A cult-like dessert among restaurateurs, it has eclipsed tiramisu's star.
A fresh dessert with vanilla seeds dotting the white jelly.

Serves 6

* * *

1 tbsp (15 ml)
plain gelatin (1 packet)

—

1 vanilla bean

—

1 1/4 cups (310 ml)
15% or 35% cream

—

1/2 cup (125 ml) sugar

—

1 3/4 cups (425 ml)
buttermilk or, if unavailable,
plain yogurt

* * *

Bloom gelatin in 2 tbsp (30 ml)
cold water for 5 minutes.

—

Split vanilla bean in two with
a knife and remove seeds.

—

Heat cream and vanilla seeds.
Add sugar and stir to dissolve.

—

Add rehydrated gelatin and stir
to dissolve completely.

—

Remove from heat and
add buttermilk.

—

Pour into six oiled ramekins
or dessert glasses.

—

Refrigerate for at least 2 hours
or until mixture sets.

—

To release panna cotta from
ramekins, run a knife around edges
and set ramekins in boiling water
for a few seconds to loosen.

* * *

Serve

*With passion fruit, a small fruit
with crunchy seeds and exquisite
flavour. Plan on one fruit per person.
Choose fruit with wrinkled skins.
Open them and use their seeds
to garnish the panna cotta.*

—

*With a strawberry or raspberry
coulis (p. 173). Surround panna cotta
with coulis and add mango cubes.*

—

*With a fruit salad. On a deep plate,
unmould panna cotta and surround it
with fruit salad. Or arrange drained
fruit salad over panna cotta in
a dessert glass.*

Berry Cheese Mousse

The cheesecake, revisited.

Serves 6

* * *

1/2 cup (125 ml)
35% whipping cream

—

8 oz (250 g)
cream cheese,
at room temperature

—

1/2 cup (125 ml)
sour cream

—

1/3 to 1/2 cup
(80 to 125 ml) sugar

—

1 tbsp (15 ml)
grated lemon zest

—

2 tbsp (30 ml)
lemon juice

—

Fresh or frozen berries
(blueberries, raspberries or a mix)

* * *

Garnish

—

18 gingersnap, Oreo or amaretti
cookies, or graham crackers

* * *

<u>In a chilled bowl</u>, whip cream.
Set aside.

—

<u>In another bowl</u>, beat cream cheese.

—

<u>Blend</u> in sour cream, sugar, lemon
zest and juice. Continue beating
until thoroughly blended.

—

<u>With a spatula</u>, fold whipped cream
into sour cream mixture.

—

<u>Pour</u> mixture into parfait glasses,
alternating with selected fruit.

—

<u>Refrigerate</u> for a few hours.

* * *

Serve
As is with a few cookies, or sprinkle
cookie crumbs over mousse.

Lychee Frozen Yogurt

Easy, light, subtle, surprising...

Serves 6 to 8

* * *

2 cans (each 19 oz / 540 ml)
lychees (around 50 lychees)

—

1/4 cup (60 ml) sugar

—

3/4 cup (180 ml) 10% yogurt

* * *

<u>Drain</u> lychees and combine
with sugar in food processor.

—

<u>Process</u> to a purée and add yogurt;
mix, taking care to scrape sides of
bowl.

—

<u>Pour</u> into a resealable plastic bag,
flatten and place in freezer.

—

<u>Let</u> harden.

—

<u>Break</u> frozen mixture into small
pieces; process once again into a
purée, pulsing and scraping sides
of bowl with a spatula.

—

<u>Leave</u> processor running until desired
consistency is achieved.

* * *

Serve
As is or garnished with fresh,
unpeeled lychees or
a crispy biscuit or brittle.

Store
In freezer for 10 days. If the
texture is too icy, return to processor
to lighten the consistency.

Mandarin Sorbet

Tasty and refreshing,
this recipe can be made in a flash and sweetened to taste.

Serves 4 to 6

* * *

2 cans (each 10 oz / 284 ml) mandarins or clementines

—

2 to 3 tsp (10 to 15 ml) finely grated ginger

—

2 tbsp (30 ml) superfine or granulated sugar

—

1 or 2 egg whites

* * *

Pour contents of mandarin cans into a resealable plastic bag. Freeze flat until very firm.

—

Just before serving, break fruit ice into pieces into food processor bowl.

—

Add ginger and sugar and pulse. Then, let processor run to thoroughly emulsify the sorbet.

—

An egg white or two will help emulsify the sorbet.

* * *

Serve

In cups or glasses. Stick a honey-sesame biscuit or chocolate square into the sorbet

—

With brittle (see below)

—

Or garnish with a few sticks of crystallized ginger

Note

The leftover egg yolks may be used to make mayonnaise (p. 178).

Rice Knispie Brittle

Adds a little crunch.
This brittle gives simple ice cream, sorbet or mousse a bit of style.

Serves 6

* * *

1/4 cup (60 ml) honey or corn syrup

—

1 cup (250 ml) Rice Krispies

—

1/2 cup (125 ml) pistachios, coarsely chopped, or slivered almonds

—

Finely grated orange zest

* * *

Preheat oven to 350°F (180°C).

—

Line a 10- x 15-in (25 x 38 cm) baking sheet with parchment paper.

—

In a small saucepan, heat honey just until liquefied.

—

In a bowl, mix Rice Krispies, pistachios and orange zest with a fork and stir in syrup.

Spread mixture on baking sheet and place in centre of oven. After 4 or 5 minutes, remove from oven. Cover brittle with waxed paper or parchment paper and, using a rolling pin or spatula, spread as thinly as possible. Cook for another 4 to 5 minutes.

—

Remove from oven and cool completely.

—

Break into pieces.

* * *

Serve

Stuck into yogurt, ice cream, sorbet or mousse

Citrus Jelly

*Fruit that is almost in its natural state,
yet fresher and more attractive.*

Serves 6 to 8

* * *

7 or 8 navel or
blood oranges

—

3 or 4 pink grapefruit

—

1/4 cup (60 ml)
honey or sugar,
more or less depending
on sweetness of fruit

—

2 tbsp (30 ml)
plain gelatin (2 packets)

* * *

Peel oranges and grapefruit closely
over a sieve and divide into segments
(p. 170).

—

Drain fruit to get 3 to 4 cups (750 ml
to 1 l) fruit and 1 1/2 cups (375 ml)
juice, adding more juice if necessary.

—

In a bowl, dissolve honey in juice.
Set aside.

—

In a small saucepan, sprinkle
gelatin over 1/4 cup (60 ml) of the
juice. Let bloom for 5 minutes.

—

Over low heat, melt gelatin and
add to reserved juice.

—

Divide fruit into glasses or
dessert cups.

—

Pour gelatin mixture over fruit, cover
with plastic wrap and chill for 5 hours
or until gelatin sets.

* * *

Variations
*Replace citrus juices with
white grape juice (Muscat) or
a good sparkling wine.*

—

*Add about 1 tsp (5 ml)
orange blossom water or 1/4 cup
(60 ml) orange liqueur to juice.*

—

Add snipped mint leaves to juice.

Kid-Friendly Fruit Juice Jelly

To please my friends who are parents,
who don't always have time to bake cookies with the kids.

✡ ✡ ✡

• 4 Tbsp (60 ml) plain gelatin (4 packets)

• 4 cups (1 l) fruit juice

to taste:

orange, cranberry, white or red grape, nectar

✡ ✡ ✡

In a bowl, bloom gelatin in 1 cup (250 ml) fruit juice for about 5 minutes

In a saucepan, heat remaining fruit juice to the boiling point, add hydrated gelatin and stir to dissolve. Pour mixture into a square 9 in (23 cm) pan.

Let set in refrigerator for at least 3 hours or overnight. To loosen jelly, set pan in hot water for a few seconds and invert onto a plate. Cut shapes in jelly with cookie cutters.

Justin Tousignant
7 and a half years old

Grapes with Port

*With drinks, with cheese, at the end of a meal...
whenever you're in the mood for them!*

* * *

1 lb (500 g)
seedless grapes

—

5 long strips lemon zest

—

1 cup (250 ml)
port or Muscat wine

* * *

Transfer grapes and lemon zest to a
medium freezer bag and pour in port.

—

Close bag and, using a straw, remove
as much air as possible to submerge
grapes in wine.

—

Let macerate for at least 6 to 8 hours
in the refrigerator. Place in a glass to
nibble after a meal. Serve chilled.

* * *

Iced Grapes

*More of a tip than a recipe—
miniature sorbets.*

* * *

Remove grapes from stem and
arrange on a large rimmed baking
sheet. Freeze for 2 to 3 hours or
until frozen. Serve grapes in a glass
to nibble.

* * *

Affogato

Affogato means ice cream drowned in coffee.
A meeting between two Italian delicacies: caffè and gelato.

* * *

Vanilla, coffee or
chocolate ice cream

—

Good, hot espresso

* * *

<u>In a cup</u> or glass mug, place a scoop
of ice cream and pour the hot
espresso over the ice cream.

—

<u>Take</u> your time savouring the
hot-cold mix.

* * *

Poached Pears with Spiced Honey

What a pleasure to combine spice with fruit.

/ 146

Serves 4

* * *

4 pears, Bosc or
other firm variety

—

1/2 cup (125 ml) honey

—

4 long strips lemon or orange zest

—

2 tbsp (30 ml)
lemon juice

—

2 star anise

—

10 peppercorns

—

1 vanilla bean, split lengthwise
and seens scraped out,
or 1 tsp (5 ml) vanilla

—

1 chili pepper

—

Water

* * *

Peel pears and, leaving stems intact,
core using a melon baller or knife.
Set pears aside in lemon water.

—

In a saucepan, combine honey,
lemon zest and juice, star anise,
peppercorns, vanilla bean (if using)
and chili pepper. If using vanilla
instead of a vanilla bean, add it only
at the end of cooking.

—

Lay pears in saucepan and add about
3 cups (750 ml) water or just enough
to cover. Cover with a disk of
parchment paper or saucepan lid.

—

Bring to a boil.

—

Reduce heat and simmer, turning
pears often, until tender but not soft,
15 to 20 minutes.

—

Add vanilla if not using vanilla bean.
Refrigerate in syrup until chilled.

* * *

Serve

Cold or at room temperature
with plain yogurt

—

With ice cream or mascarpone
cheese thinned with a little syrup

—

With Chocolate Sauce (p. 170)

Store

In season, you can make a large
batch and divide it into containers
to keep in the refrigerator or to offer
as gifts. Leave spices in syrup
for decoration.

Cardamom Buttons

*A deliciously aromatic shortbread that my cousin Chantal
likes to give us every Christmas.*

48 shortbreads

* * *

3/4 cup (180 ml)
butter, at room temperature

—

2/3 cup (160 ml)
brown sugar

—

1/4 cup (60 ml)
15% cream

—

1 1/2 cups (375 ml) flour

—

2 tsp (10 ml)
ground cardamom

—

1/2 tsp (2 ml)
baking powder

—

1/2 tsp (2 ml)
baking soda

—

Generous pinch of salt

* * *

In a bowl, using an electric mixer
or a spoon, beat butter and brown
sugar until creamy. Add cream and
combine.

—

In another bowl, sift flour, cardamom,
baking powder, baking soda and salt.
Combine with butter mixture.

Divide dough into two equal parts.

On a sheet of plastic wrap, form
two rolls, each 12 in (30 cm) long
by 1 in (2.5 cm) in diameter. Wrap
carefully in plastic wrap and then
in foil.

—

Freeze for at least 1 hour.

Preheat oven to 375°F (190°C).

—

Cut dough into 3/8-in (1 cm) slices.
Using a chopstick, make two holes
in each and place slices on a
baking sheet.

Bake for about 8 minutes.
Cool on a rack.

* * *

Store
*Dough will keep for months in
the freezer. Make sure to always
have these shortbreads handy to
serve with pastries, chocolates
and berries, or with ice cream
and sorbet.*

Truffle Squares

This recipe falls somewhere between crafts and cooking.
The humble mould for so noble a delicacy—a clean milk carton.
This recipe makes 16 little chocolate squares to serve at the end of a meal with biscuits,
nougat, and fresh or dried berries.

/ 150

16 small squares

* * *

1/4 cup (60 ml)
35% cream
—
4 oz (120 g)
semisweet chocolate,
finely chopped
—
1 tsp (5 ml) butter
—
Cocoa powder

* * *

Cut out the bottom of a 1 l milk carton, leaving an edge 1 in (2.5 cm) high.

—

If needed, cut a second bottom of the same size to obtain a smooth surface.

—

Line the bottom of the carton with a double layer of plastic wrap, making sure there is enough wrap to overhang edges to make it easy to unmould.

—

Pour cream into a saucepan and bring to a boil. Remove from heat and add chocolate. Add butter and stir with a wooden spoon to melt chocolate completely.

—

Pour ganache into mould. Cover mould with plastic wrap and refrigerate for a few hours until ganache is completely chilled.

—

Unmould, remove plastic wrap and, if necessary, smooth surface using a long knife dipped in boiling water and wiped dry.

—

To make slicing easier, run knife under hot water and wipe dry before cutting into sixteen 1/2-in (1.5 cm) squares.

—

Dust tops of squares with cocoa.

* * *

With Alcohol

* * *

Blend 1 tbsp (15 ml) Bailey's, Grand Marnier, rum, Pernod or brandy into ganache before pouring into mould.

* * *

With Fresh Mint

* * *

The flavour of fresh mint takes these miles away from After Eight chocolates. Infuse 1/3 cup (80 ml) chopped fresh mint leaves in 1/3 cup (80 ml) heated cream for 1 hour. Reheat cream and strain before adding chopped chocolate. Stir until chocolate melts.

* * *

With Bergamot Tea

* * *

Infuse 1 Earl Grey tea bag in heated cream for 15 minutes. Squeeze tea bag to extract as much of the flavour as possible and strain cream to remove bits of tea leaves. Reheat cream and add to chocolate, stirring until melted.

* * *.

Almond, Chocolate and Date Cake

For the holidays, roasted almonds, good chocolate and dates:
my father's favourite cake.

16 squares

* * *

1 2/3 cups (410 ml)
almonds

—

8 oz (250 g)
semisweet chocolate,
coarsely chopped

—

6 egg whites

—

1/4 cup (60 ml) sugar

—

8 oz (250 g) or
2 cups (500 ml)
dates, pitted and finely chopped

* * *

Garnish

—

Fresh or whipped cream

—

Cocoa

* * *

Preheat oven to 350°F (180°C).

—

On a baking sheet, toast
almonds lightly, 7 to 8 minutes.
Cool completely.

—

Butter a 9-in (23 cm) square cake
pan and line with parchment paper.

—

Pulse almonds and chocolate
in a food processor until coarsely
chopped. Set aside.

—

In a large bowl, beat egg whites,
adding the sugar a little at a time,
until firm peaks form.

—

Using a spatula, gently fold in
almond mixture and dates.

—

Pour into pan.

—

Bake for 40 to 45 minutes.

—

Let rest at room temperature
in pan until completely cooled.

—

Unmould cake onto a plate and
refrigerate overnight.

—

Cut cake into squares and garnish
to taste.

* * *

Serve
Warm or at room temperature.

Note
Egg yolks keep, refrigerated,
for up to 3 days in a tightly
closed container. Use them in:

—

Mayonnaise (p. 178)

—

Spaghetti Carbonara

—

Crème anglaise

—

Crème caramel

—

Pudding, etc.

Store
In refrigerator,
in a tightly closed container.

Chocolate Cream Shots

A jewel of a recipe that my friend Michelle Gélinas has been making for ages.
It's been slightly revisited with a different flavour.
A small portion brings great happiness! The better the chocolate, the better…

/ 154

Serves 6 to 8

* * *

3/4 cup (180 ml)
10% cream or whole milk

—

5 to 6 oz (150 to 180 g)
semisweet chocolate

—

3 tbsp (45 ml) hot espresso
or very strong coffee

—

3 eggs

—

2 tbsp (30 ml)
alcohol (rum, cognac, or
coffee or orange liqueur)
or coffee

* * *

Garnishes, to taste

—

Lightly whipped cream

—

Chocolate-covered
coffee beans

—

Cocoa powder

—

Chunks of fresh fruit

* * *

Heat cream to the boiling point.

—

In a blender or food processor, chop chocolate.

—

With processor running, add hot coffee, eggs and alcohol.

—

With processor still running, pour in boiling cream in a thin stream.

—

Fill espresso cups, glasses or small tea cups with 1/3 cup (80 ml) each.

—

Refrigerate for at least 2 hours.

—

Garnish as desired.

* * *

With Cardamom

* * *

Infuse 1/4 tsp (1 ml) ground cardamom in heated cream or milk until flavoured. Reheat to the boiling point and strain, pouring boiling liquid into blender or food processor bowl.

Steamed Spiced Chocolate Pudding

A classic holiday dish, with a non-traditional twist.
Spice, coffee and chocolate flavours meld together in this steamed pudding.
Another enormous advantage of this pudding is that it can be made in advance.

/ 156

Serves 8

* * *

4 oz (120 g)
semisweet chocolate, chopped
—
1/2 cup (125 ml) butter
—
2 eggs
—
1/2 cup (125 ml)
packed brown sugar
—
1 tbsp (15 ml)
finely grated orange zest
—
1/4 cup (60 ml)
orange juice
—
1 cup (250 ml) flour
—
1 1/2 tsp (7 ml)
baking powder
—
1 1/2 tsp (7 ml)
ground ginger
—
1 tsp (5 ml)
ground cinnamon
—
1/2 tsp (2 ml)
freshly ground pepper
—
1/2 tsp (2 ml)
dry mustard
—
1/2 cup (125 ml)
cold strong coffee
—
1 tbsp (15 ml) vanilla

* * *

Generously butter a 4-cup (1 l)
steamed pudding mould with a tight-
fitting lid*.
—
Melt chocolate and butter in
a double-boiler. Stir regularly until
chocolate has completely melted.
—
Remove from heat and let cool for
a few minutes.
—
In bowl, combine eggs and brown
sugar until blended.
—
Stir chocolate mixture into egg
mixture.
—
Add orange zest and juice.
—
Sift flour, baking powder, ginger,
cinnamon, pepper and mustard over
chocolate and fold in just enough to
moisten. Stir in strong coffee and
vanilla.
—
Pour mixture into mould and cover.
—
Place mould in a pan of hot water,
making sure water reaches halfway
up sides of mould.
—

Cover pan and bring water to a boil.
Reduce heat to simmer.
—
Cook for about 1 1/2 hours.
During cooking time, add hot water
as needed to maintain water level.
—
Unmould pudding onto a serving
platter and serve hot or warm.

* * *

Serve
With good vanilla ice cream,
slightly softened in the refrigerator
—
Topped with crème anglaise or a
drizzle of Chocolate Sauce (p. 170)

Note
To reheat pudding, place mould
in a casserole dish. Pour water into
dish until halfway up side of mould.
Reduce heat to the lowest setting and
reheat, covered, for 30 to 40 minutes.

*If you don't have a traditional mould with a lid,
use a metal bowl or a high-sided earthenware
mould. Cover with buttered foil and secure with
a string.

Chocolate Birthday Cake

*On the show we were all mad for the Cluny chocolate cake.
We now enjoy it at every birthday.
In addition to being succulent, it serves at least 16.*

Serves 16

* * *

8 oz (250 g)
semisweet chocolate,
coarsely chopped

—

1/2 cup (125 ml)
unsalted butter

—

1 cup (250 ml)
boiling water

—

3 eggs

—

2 cups (500 ml) sugar

—

2 tsp (10 ml) vanilla

—

1/2 cup (125 ml)
sour cream

—

1 tsp (5 ml)
baking soda

—

2 cups (500 ml) flour

—

1/2 cup (125 ml) cocoa powder

—

1 1/2 tsp (7 ml)
baking powder

—

1/2 tsp (2 ml) salt

* * *

<u>Preheat</u> oven to 350°F (180°C).

—

<u>Generously butter</u> and flour
a tube pan.

—

<u>In a double boiler</u>, melt 6 oz (180 g)
of the chocolate with the butter.
Add boiling water and stir to combine.
Set aside.

—

<u>In a large bowl</u>, beat eggs, sugar and
vanilla. Set aside.

—

<u>In another bowl</u>, beat sour cream and
baking soda. Set aside.

—

<u>In a large bowl</u>, mix flour, cocoa,
baking powder and salt. Set aside.

—

<u>Add</u> egg mixture to chocolate mixture.

—

<u>Pour</u> chocolate mixture over dry
ingredients, combining with a spoon,
then beat to mix thoroughly.

—

<u>Stir</u> in sour cream mixture and
remaining chopped chocolate.

—

<u>Pour</u> into prepared pan.

—

<u>Bake</u> for about 50 minutes or until
a knife inserted in cake comes out
clean. Unmould cake onto a rack
and cool.

—

<u>Gently pour</u> ganache (see right)
over cake.

* * *

Ganache

* * *

1/2 cup (125 ml)
35% cream

—

6 oz (180 g)
semisweet chocolate, chopped

* * *

<u>In a saucepan</u>, bring cream to a boil.

—

<u>Place</u> chocolate in a bowl and
add boiling cream.

—

<u>Stir</u> until chocolate is melted. Cool
at room temperature until ganache
thickens slightly.

* * *

Apple-Pecan Crisp

*The "À la di Stasio" episode was barely over
when the team threw themselves at the small, still-warm bowls of this crisp!*

Serves 6

* * *

6 large apples,
peeled, seeded and chopped
(Golden, Cortland,
Braeburn or Rome Beauty)

—

1/4 cup (60 ml)
packed brown sugar or
maple syrup

—

2 tbsp (30 ml)
cornstarch

—

Juice of 1 lemon

* * *

Crisp

—

2 cups (500 ml)
pecans, coarsely chopped

—

6 tbsp (90 ml) flour

—

1/2 cup (125 ml)
packed brown sugar

—

6 tbsp (90 ml)
butter, softened

* * *

<u>Preheat</u> oven to 350°F (180°C).

—

<u>In a bowl</u>, mix apples, brown sugar,
cornstarch and lemon juice.

—

<u>Pour</u> into six 1-cup (250 ml) ramekins
or a square 9-in (23 cm) pan.

—

<u>Combine</u> pecans, flour, brown sugar
and butter and spread over apples.

—

<u>Cook</u> individual crisps for 30 to
35 minutes or large single crisp for
35 to 40 minutes.

* * *

Serve
*Hot or warm, with vanilla
ice cream, 10% yogurt or
heavy cream*

Note
*Crisp ingredients can
also be blended by pulsing in
a food processor.*

Variation
*Add cinnamon,
nutmeg, allspice or finely chopped
fresh rosemary to apple mixture
to taste.*

Mango and Frangipane Tarts

With mangoes or pears,
square or round, in the afternoon or in the evening,
these tarts are always good.

Serves 4

* * *

Frangipane*
—
1/4 cup (60 ml)
butter, at room temperature
—
1/4 cup (60 ml) sugar
—
1 egg
—
1/2 cup (125 ml)
ground almonds
—
1/4 tsp (1 ml)
almond extract

* * *

Crust
—
7 oz (200 g)
store-bought puff pastry
(1/2 package)
—
3 mangoes
—
1 tbsp (15 ml)
sugar (optional)

* * *

To make frangipane, in a bowl, beat butter and sugar with electric beater until mixture is light and creamy. Add egg and beat until blended. Stir in ground almonds and almond extract. Set aside.

—

Preheat oven to 400°F (200°C).

—

Line a baking sheet with parchment paper or foil.

—

On a lightly floured surface, roll out pastry to 1/8 in (3 mm) thickness.

—

Using an overturned side plate as a guide, cut pastry into four 6-in (15 cm) rounds.

—

Place pastry rounds on baking sheet. Pierce all over with a fork. Set aside in freezer or refrigerate for up to 1 hour.

—

Wash mangoes, score skin and, using a vegetable peeler, peel. Trim flesh as close as possible to the pit. Slice flesh.

—

Spread frangipane evenly over each pastry round.

Arrange mango slices in a circular pattern, overlapping, over frangipane. Sprinkle fruit with sugar, if desired.

—

Bake for 15 to 20 minutes or until mangoes are golden and the bottom of the crust is cooked.

* * *

Serve
Warm

Variation
Substitute pears for mangoes. Peel, cut in half, remove core with a melon baller and slice before arranging on top of frangipane.

*The frangipane can be replaced with 1/2 cup (125 ml) almond paste, grated. Use 2 tbsp (30 ml) per tart.

Lemon Soufflé Cake

*The texture of a soufflé with sauce underneath makes this cake irresistible.
A must for lemon aficionados.*

Serves 6 to 8

* * *

4 eggs, separated

—

Pinch salt

—

1 cup (250 ml) sugar

—

1/2 cup (125 ml)
butter, at room temperature

—

1/2 cup (125 ml) flour

—

Grated zest of 2 lemons

—

1/3 cup (80 ml)
lemon juice

—

1 1/2 cups (375 ml) milk

* * *

Preheat oven to 375°F (190°C).

—

Butter a large 6-cup (1.5 l) soufflé
dish and place it in a 9- x 13-in
(23 x 33 cm) baking pan.

—

In a large bowl, using an electric
mixer, beat egg whites with salt
until soft peaks form.

—

Beat, adding 1/4 cup (60 ml) sugar,
a little at a time, until meringue is
firm and glossy, about 5 minutes.
Set aside.

—

In a medium bowl, cream butter and
remaining sugar with electric mixer
for 2 minutes or until mixture is light
and creamy. Add egg yolks, one at a
time, beating after each addition.

—

Sift flour over butter mixture.
Continue to beat until batter is
well blended and smooth.

—

Add lemon zest and juice, then milk.
Combine well.

—

Fold in egg whites using a spatula.

—

Pour into dish. Pour boiling water
into baking pan until halfway up sides
of soufflé dish.

Bake for 35 to 40 minutes or until
top of cake is golden and cake is
nearly set.

—

Let cool for 10 minutes before
serving.

* * *

*Note
Serving-size portions of
this dessert can be reheated in
the microwave.*

Caramel Spread

I was always afraid to make caramel.
Chef Mustapha Rougaibi made some on the show; I gave in and started making it for all my friends.
This may be the only recipe in this book that requires a little more attention.
Candy making being what it is, care is required—but it's so good!

Makes five 8-oz (250 ml) jars

* * *

2 cups (500 ml) sugar

—

1/2 cup (125 ml)
white corn syrup

—

3 1/3 cups (830 ml)
35% cream, heated

—

3/4 lb (360 g)
salted butter, softened

—

2 tsp (10 ml)
Guérande salt or
fleur de sel (optional)

* * *

<u>Fill</u> the bottom of the sink with cold water.

—

<u>In a heavy</u> 20-cup (5 l) saucepan, mix sugar and corn syrup.

—

<u>Cook</u> caramel over medium heat, stirring, until mixture reaches 365°F (185°C) to 374°F (190°C) on a candy thermometer. If needed, remove pan from heat.

—

This is the crucial step. Be vigilant, as the temperature rises very quickly. As soon as the temperature is reached, immerse bottom of saucepan into cold water to stop cooking process.

—

<u>If the temperature is too high</u> and the caramel is too dark, there is nothing to be done except start again from scratch, as the caramel would be too bitter.

—

<u>Add</u> hot cream to caramel, a little at a time, stirring. **Caution! This can splatter.**

—

<u>The temperature will drop</u>.

—

<u>Continue</u> cooking until caramel reaches 225°F (107°C) on candy thermometer, stirring.

—

<u>Cool</u> to 86 to 104°F (30 to 40°C).

—

<u>Stir</u> in butter vigorously with a wooden spoon. Add salt, if desired, and stir.

—

<u>Fill</u> jars and keep in refrigerator.

* * *

Serve
Spread on toast.

—

For a quick dessert, dip a soup spoon into caramel and stick a square of good-quality dark chocolate in it.

—

You can also pour heated caramel over fruit salad or ice cream.

Note
Making caramel is a question of habit and taste.
Feel free to vary the caramel's temperature between 365°F (185°C) and 383°F (195°C). A higher temperature will yield a more bitter caramel.

— The Basics —
Tips and Recipes

* * *

/ 170

Citrus Fruits

How to segment

* * *

First, peel fruit well. To do this, use a sharp knife to remove peel and pith as closely as possible to the flesh of the fruit.

—

Then slip the knife between the fruit and the fine membranes, separating the segments, and remove carefully.

—

Always work over a bowl to catch juices.

* * *

Roasted Garlic

See p. 117.

* * *

Asparagus

How to prepare asparagus

* * *

To store asparagus, trim stems and set upright in a bowl half-filled with fresh water. Cover with plastic wrap and refrigerate.

—

To prepare asparagus for cooking, snap stems in half. Peel from flower to stem end with vegetable peeler.

Asparagus can be blanched in boiling salted water, steamed, or roasted in the oven or on the barbecue.

* * *

Cranberries

Cranberry Sauce

*Makes approximately
2 cups (500 ml)*

* * *

1/3 cup (80 ml)
fresh mint leaves, chopped

—

1 bag (10 1/2 oz / 300 g)
fresh or frozen cranberries

—

Zest of 1 orange, finely grated

—

1 cup (250 ml) orange juice

—

1/2 cup (125 ml) sugar

* * *

In a saucepan, bring mint, cranberries, orange zest and juice, and sugar to a boil, stirring frequently.

—

Reduce heat and simmer for 10 minutes or until cranberries start to burst. Cool.

—

Pour into a bowl, cover tightly and refrigerate.

* * *

Chocolate

Ganache

See p. 158.

* * *

Chocolate Syrup

Makes 3/4 cup (180 ml)

* * *

1/2 cup (125 ml) sugar

—

1/4 cup (60 ml) cocoa powder

—

1/2 cup (125 ml) water

—

2 oz (60 g) semisweet
chocolate, chopped

* * *

In a small saucepan, blend sugar and cocoa. Add water and chopped chocolate.

—

Heat over medium heat, stirring constantly, until chocolate is melted.

—

Syrup can be made ahead of time, refrigerated, and reheated as needed.

* * *

Chocolate Sauce

Makes 3/4 cup (180 ml)

* * *

4 oz (120 g)
semisweet chocolate,
coarsely chopped

—

1/2 cup (125 ml)
35% cream

* * *

In a heatproof bowl set over saucepan of simmering water, melt chocolate with cream, stirring occasionally.

—

Pour into a bowl, cool and refrigerate, covered.

—

Heat before serving.

* * *

Croutons

Bruschetta or Crostini

* * *

Bruschetta are largish slices of rustic, country-style bread. The bread is toasted under the boiler or in a toaster and rubbed, or not, with a half-clove of garlic when warm. The bread slices are then garnished with Pepperonata (p. 120) or another savoury topping.

—

Crostini are smaller: cut square bread into quarters, or slice thin (ficelle) or regular baguette. Toasted, they are used as a base for canapés.

* * *

Toasted Baguette or Ficelle

* * *

Preheat oven to 350°F (180°C).

—

Slice bread diagonally or crosswise. Lay out on a baking sheet and toast for about 15 minutes or until bread is golden brown.

* * *

Diced Croutons

* * *

It is easier to cut bread into cubes when it is not too fresh.

—

These croutons cannot be compared with those generally found in the market. Drop them onto salads and into soups.

* * *

4 cups (1 l)
evenly diced bread, crusts removed,
1/2- to 1-in (1 to 2.5 cm) pieces

—

1/4 cup (60 ml)
olive oil or melted butter, or equal parts of each

—

Salt and freshly ground pepper

—

Grated Parmesan, spices, herbs or crushed garlic (optional)

* * *

Preheat oven to 350°F (180°C).

—

In a bowl, combine bread with oil. Add salt and pepper. Season as desired.

—

Arrange croutons in a single layer on baking sheet. Cook for about 15 minutes or until croutons are golden brown, shaking the sheet a few times during cooking time.

* * *

Pita Croutons

* * *

These croutons are actually better than chips! They are perfect with hummus and other spreads, and Middle Eastern soups, or crumbled into salads.

* * *

Medium pita breads,
about 7 in (18 cm) in diameter

—

Olive oil

—

Sea salt

—

Pepper

Spices, to taste

Zaatar (a thyme-and-sesame-based blend found in Middle Eastern stores), curry powder, paprika, oregano

or

Replace salt with celery salt or lemon salt

* * *

Preheat oven to 350°F (180°C).

—

Open each pita and separate into two parts. Brush with oil and season to taste.

—

Stack pitas and cut into 8 wedges.

—

Arrange on a baking sheet and toast for about 8 minutes.

—

Or open pitas and leave whole, brush with oil, season and toast until croutons are golden brown.

* * *

Spices

To bring out the flavour

* * *

It is important to heat spices lightly to release their essential oils.

—

After heating, grind spices using a mortar and pestle, or coffee grinder.

—

To clean the coffee grinder, add 2 tbsp (30 ml) coarse salt and run grinder while shaking it. Discard salt and wipe out grinder with a damp cloth. Let air-dry for about 10 minutes.

* * *

Fennel

How to prepare fennel

* * *

Cut off fennel stems and remove first outside leaf if wilted. Using a vegetable peeler, peel the outside of the bulb to remove strings, or remove strings individually with a paring knife.

—

To prepare for cooking, cut bulb in half through the centre without damaging the heart, which holds leaves in place. Then cut into wedges, leaving leaves attached to heart.

—

Fennel is delicious raw, cut into sticks and served with olive oil or tapenade. It is also eaten shredded and in salads.

—

Cooked, it is delicious gently braised in stock. Avoid overcooking.

* * *

Strawberries and Raspberries

Strawberry or Raspberry Coulis

Makes 1 cup (250 ml)

* * *

1 container
(10 1/2 oz / 300 g) frozen
strawberries or raspberries, thawed

—

1/4 cup (60 ml) sugar

—

1 tsp (5 ml) lemon juice

* * *

Place strawberries, sugar and lemon juice in blender or food processor and reduce to a purée. Be sure to scrape sides of bowl.

—

If using raspberries, strain through a sieve to remove seeds.

* * *

Cheese

Serving Ideas

* * *

Some people are less dessert-oriented and prefer to finish a meal with some cheese. In any case, we are proud to present good domestic cheeses as well as the newest imports. We can sit around the table without having to cook. To fully enjoy cheeses with your guests, don't serve too heavy a meal, otherwise the cheese will be all yours the next day!

—

If using more than one cheese, balance textures and flavours. Personally, I prefer to serve a single type. It's nice to serve a big piece of cheese with a well-paired accompaniment.

With Fruit

* * *

As with the rest of the meal, go with the season. Berries, strawberries or other varieties, pair well with fresh cheeses. Serve apples in season with Cheddar or mould-ripened cheese. Or try fresh figs, pears, etc.

* * *

With Nuts

* * *

Roast nuts on a baking sheet at 350°F (180°C) for 8 to 10 minutes. Or serve whole nuts that are fun to crack.

* * *

With Dried Fruit

* * *

Serve dried fruit plain or alcohol-soaked. Or try a fruit pâté, such as quince pâté, often served in Spain and delicious with Manchego cheese or over parsley noodles.

* * *

In Salads

* * *

Add fruit such as pears or figs. If you have some nut oil, add a few drops to your dressing and sprinkle some roasted nuts on the salad.

* * *

With Bread

* * *

Try crackers, biscotti and especially homemade bread. Thick crust, soft bread, raisin bread, nut bread, and even focaccia go with some cheeses.

* * *

Cheese Leftovers

* * *

_ Think deluxe grilled cheese (p. 108). Good bread, good cheese and a filling—sautéed mushrooms, sun-dried tomato pesto, fresh arugula, etc.

_ Melt cheese onto a crouton and place this delicious assembly on top of soup.

_ Grate leftover cheese to make vegetable or pasta gratin.

_ Mix it into a tomato or green salad.

_ Use as an omelette filling.

_ Use to cover a pizza.

_ In the case of a blue cheese, blend it with a little butter and serve on grilled beef or veal, or baked potatoes.

_ Add Parmesan or grana Padano rind to a soup such as Minestrone (p. 42).

* * *

Oil

* * *

I strongly suggest finding good olive oils and using them raw, as a condiment on the table. It's a matter of remembering to do it. Serve with raw and cooked vegetables, soups, salads, mashes, roasts, fish and rice. There are also excellent flavoured oils on the market, but making your own is very gratifying.

Lemon Oil

* * *

Perfect for dipping good, crusty bread, raw vegetables or artichoke leaves. This oil is also delicious on salads, fish or cooked vegetables. Having tried several different methods — heat infusions, long-term cold infusions, etc. — this one is the best.

* * *

Makes 1 cup (250 ml)

* * *

4 lemons,
preferably organic

—

2 pinches salt

—

1 cup (250 ml)
olive oil

* * *

Thoroughly scrub lemons and remove zest. I use a rasp. The main thing is to avoid the white pith, which makes the oil bitter.

—

Place two good pinches of salt in a mortar or bowl and crush the zest into the salt to extract the oil. This step is worth the time. Cover the zest with olive oil and let steep for at least 7 hours, or to taste. Line a sieve with a paper towel and strain the oil into a clean container.

—

Keeps for several weeks in the refrigerator.

* * *

Pepper Oil

Makes 1 cup (250 ml)

* * *

1 cup (250 ml)
olive or other oil

—

1/4 cup (60 ml)
hot pepper flakes or
small hot peppers, crushed

—

1 garlic clove, peeled

—

1 bay leaf (optional)

—

Herbes de Provence (optional)

* * *

Gently heat oil in saucepan, without boiling.

—

Add pepper and garlic to oil. Remove from heat.

—

Set aside in a jar and let macerate for a few days before tasting. (Be careful with garlic in oil; read safety note on p. 117) When flavours peak, strain oil through a sieve lined with a paper towel.

—

Pour oil into a small bottle. Do not include garlic clove. If you like, add a bay leaf or herbes de Provence.

—

Use on pastas, pizzas, soups and stir-fries.

—

Keep in refrigerator.

* * *

Vegetables
How to prepare vegetables

* * *

See Asparagus (p. 170);
Lemongrass (p. 66); Fennel (p. 173);
Peppers (p. 179); Tomatoes (p. 179).

* * *

Mangoes
How to peel and cut mangoes

* * *

See p. 32.

* * *

Mayonnaise
Makes 2 cups (500 ml)

* * *

2 egg yolks or 1 egg
—
2 to 3 tsp (10 to 15 ml)
Dijon mustard
—
Salt and freshly ground pepper
—
1 to 2 tbsp (15 to 30 ml)
white wine vinegar or lemon juice
—
1/3 cup (80 ml) olive oil
—
1 cup (250 ml) canola oil

* * *

In a bowl, whisk egg yolks, mustard, pepper and vinegar.
—
While whisking, pour in olive oil a few drops at a time, then blend in canola oil in one thin stream. Whisk vigorously until desired texture is obtained*.

* * *

Note

To prepare mayonnaise in a blender, add olive oil to egg yolk mixture. Blend. Add canola oil in a thin stream.

* * *

*If mayonnaise is too thick, thin it with a few drops of hot water, fruit juice or Pernod. If the mayonnaise separates, start over with a clean bowl containing one egg yolk and Dijon mustard, whisking in small spoonfuls of the original mixture until blended. Continue as indicated above.

Olives
How to pit olives

* * *

See p. 14.

* * *

Oranges and Grapefruit

See Citrus Fruit, p. 170.

* * *

Parmesan
How to make Parmesan shards

* * *

To make shards: Parmesan is easier to work with when it is at room temperature. Using a vegetable peeler or cheese slicer on a smooth side of the block of cheese, lift shard away in one continuous movement in the hope that the cheese "curls and rolls" under the blade. It's all in the wrist. Practice makes perfect!

* * *

Parmesan Coulis
See p. 94.

* * *

Pâte brisée

* * *

The secret of butter-based pâte brisée is to work it as little as possible. The dots of butter in the flour melt while cooking, and the steam they create raise the dough, making it very flaky.

* * *

Makes 2 crusts, 9 in (23 cm) each

* * *

2 cups (500 ml) flour

—

2 tbsp (30 ml) sugar*

—

Pinch salt

—

1 cup (250 ml) cold butter, cubed**

—

1/3 cup (80 ml) ice water

* * *

In food processor, blend flour, sugar and salt for approximately 15 seconds. Distribute butter evenly over flour mixture, pulsing until the butter particles are reduced to the size of small peas.

—

Add water, pulsing, until dough forms a ball. If needed, add 1 or 2 more spoonfuls of ice water.

—

Form into 2 disks, wrap in plastic wrap and refrigerate for at least 30 minutes or up to 1 hour.

—

Remove dough from refrigerator 15 minutes before using. Roll out dough, beginning at the centre of each disk.

* * *

Store

Freeze for 3 months, well wrapped in plastic and placed in a resealable freezer bag.

* * *

*Omit sugar for savoury pies.

** For a flakier crust, you may replace up to a quarter of the butter with an equivalent amount of shortening.

Peppers

How to prepare peppers

* * *

To peel peppers, cut in half, seed, coat with oil and place on a baking sheet lined with foil. Roast peppers under the broiler until skins blacken, approximately 5 minutes.

—

Remove from oven and wrap foil around peppers. The steam the peppers give off while cooling will loosen the skins. Let cool.

—

Skins will come off easily with a paring knife. You can also char peppers on the barbecue, then place them in a bowl, cover them while they cool, then peel.

* * *

Prosciutto

See Prosciutto Chips, p. 30.

* * *

Chocolate Sauce

See Chocolate, p. 170.

* * *

Cranberry Sauce

See Cranberries, p. 170.

* * *

Chocolate Syrup

See Chocolate, p. 170.

* * *

Tomatoes

How to prepare tomatoes

* * *

If the tomatoes are to be eaten cooked, they must be peeled and seeded.

—

To peel tomatoes easily, cut an X into the base of each, remove stem and immerse in boiling water for 15 seconds. Plunge into ice water. Peel. To seed, cut tomatoes in half and squeeze to extract juice and seeds.

* * *

Tomato Sauce
See p. 94.

* * *

Mint-Tomato Sauce
See p. 94.

* * *

Tomato Sauce and Parmesan Coulis
See p. 94.

* * *

À la di Stasio Menus

✳

Tasty, colourful and simple. For a quick lunch,
a Saturday evening among friends or a festive meal,
here are a few menu suggestions to guide you as you acquaint yourself
with these recipes and adapt them to your own taste.

✳

Brunch 1

* * *

Start things off
by waking up your taste buds!
For children:
Kid-Friendly Fruit Juice Jelly 142
—
Mandarin Sorbet 138
or
Citrus Jelly 140

* * *

HAM AND EGG RAMEKINS 54
with a seasonal salad or
Mexican salsa

* * *

And for dessert...
Cheese Platter 175
or
Affogato 145
or
Apple Pecan Crisp 160
or
Chocolate Birthday Cake 158

* * *

Brunch 2

* * *

For children:
Kid-Friendly Fruit
Juice Jelly 142
—
Citrus Jelly 140

* * *

CHEESE SOUFFLÉS 56
—
with Braised Beet Salad 34
or a seasonal green salad
and Roasted Asparagus 118

* * *

And for dessert...
Grapes with Port 144
or
Almond, Chocolate and
Date Cake 152
or
Apple Pecan Crisp 160

* * *

Lunch 1

* * *

Golden crisp!
GRILLED CHEESE 108
—
with a Virgin Mary

* * *

And for dessert…
Almond, Chocolate and
Date Cake 152
or
apples and pears

* * *

Lunch 2

* * *

PISSALADIÈRE 106
—
with Green Salad
with Parmesan Vinaigrette
(omit roasted onion) 30
or
Parmesan, Mushroom and
Fennel Salad 36
or
Apple and Fennel Salad 36

* * *

Lunch 3

* * *

SALMON BURGERS
Asian-Style
Salmon Patties 60
with wasabi mayonnaise
and cucumbers, served
with raw vegetables
or
Salmon Patties Dijonnaise 60
with arugula and lemon mayonnaise

* * *

And for dessert…
Chocolate Cream Shots 154
or
Mandarin Sorbet 138

* * *

Single Dish Meal

Served at the table.

* * *

CHAMPVALLON 84
—
PASTAS, PIZZAS AND
GRILLED SANDWICHES 92–109
—
HEARTY ASIAN
CHICKEN SOUP 66
—
ASIAN-STYLE PORK LOIN 80
—
CHEESY CHICKEN
WITH ROASTED VEGETABLES 68
—
DUCK AND TURKEY PIE 76
—
OSSO BUCCO WITH FENNEL
AND GREMOLATA 90

* * *

/ 181

Vegetarian Meal Ideas

* * *

PASTA CAPONATA 98
—
CHEESE-STUFFED PASTA WITH TOMATO SAUCE
AND PARMESAN COULIS 94
—
PASTA PEPE E CACIO 96
—
CHEESE SOUFFLÉS 56
—
EGG PIZZA 104
—
ONION PIZZA 106
—
PISSALADIÈRE 106
—
BAKED POLENTA 129
with Zucchini-Tomato Tian 112
or
Pepperonata 120

* * *

Quick Meals

Prepared ahead of time or at a moment's notice…
you get to eat along with your guests!

/ 182

1

* * *

Japanese Watercress Salad 35
and pan-fried mushrooms
or
Mushroom Stock 48

* * *

CATCH OF THE DAY
WITH ORANGE SAUCE 63

—

Basmati Rice 128
or
Mashed Potatoes 122
and Greens 114–115

* * *

Poached Pears
with Spiced Honey 146

* * *

2

* * *

Quick as a flash
Stracciatella 44
or
Mushroom Stock 48

* * *

DUCK CONFIT 79
with green salad

* * *

Chocolate Cream Shots 154
or
Grapes with Port 144
or
Poached Pears with Spiced Honey
146

* * *

3

* * *

Tomato-Mango Salad 32

* * *

PAN-FRIED SHRIMP
WITH GINGER EMULSION 64

—

Basmati Rice 128
and Bok Choy 114

* * *

Lychee Frozen Yogurt 136

* * *

4

* * *

Chinese Egg Drop Soup 44

* * *

ASIAN-STYLE
SALMON PATTIES 60
with Japanese Watercress Salad 35

* * *

Mandarin Sorbet 138

* * *

5

* * *

No-Cook or Low-Cook
Cocktail-Hour Platter 12

* * *

PASTA PEPE E CACIO 96

* * *

Grapes with Port 144
or
Mandarin Sorbet 138

* * *

6

* * *

Parmesan, Mushroom and
Fennel Salad 36
or
Apple and Fennel Salad 36

* * *

TURKEY CUTLETS PICCATA 72

—

Roasted Green Beans 118
and pasta with sun-dried
tomato pesto

* * *

Cheese Platter 175
or
Chocolate Cream Shots 154
or
Grapes with Port 144

* * *

7

* * *

Green Salad with
Parmesan Vinaigrette 30
or
Parmesan, Mushroom and
Fennel Salad 36

* * *

ITALIAN SAUSAGES
WITH GRAPES 82

—

Baked Polenta 129
or Mashed Potatoes 122
and Rapini 115

* * *

Affogato 145
or homemade ice cream

* * *

Saturday Night

It's always such a pleasure!

1

* * *

Mushroom Stock 48

or

Oysters 40

* * *

SPICE-RUBBED SALMON 58

—

Mashed Potatoes 122
and Braised Beet Salad 34

or

Warm Potato Salad
with Mustard 124

* * *

Always fine

Mango and Frangipane Tarts 163

* * *

2

* * *

Mushroom Stock 48
with small vegetables

or

Butternut Squash Soup 47

* * *

Guaranteed aroma

BRAISED BEEF
WITH STAR ANISE 89

—

Celeriac Mash 123
and Bok Choy 114

* * *

seasonal fruit

or

Citrus Jelly 140

* * *

3

* * *

Comfort Food!

Roasted Leeks with Mint 25

or

Green Salad with Parmesan
Vinaigrette 30

* * *

OSSO BUCCO WITH FENNEL 90

—

Baked Polenta 129

or

Mashed Potatoes 122

or

Noodles with butter
and Gremolata 90

* * *

Panna cotta 132

* * *

4

* * *

No-Cook or Low-Cook
Cocktail Hour Platter 12

or

Stracciatella 44

* * *

For any season

CHEESY CHICKEN WITH
ROASTED VEGETABLES 68
(with or without cheese)

* * *

Apple Pecan Crisp 160

* * *

5

* * *

Butternut Squash Soup 47

* * *

A classic

CHAMPVALLON 84

—

with Green Salad

* * *

Grapes with Port 144

or

Poached Pears
with Spiced Honey 146

* * *

6

*A meal centred around
a braised dish*

* * *

Pepperonata 120

or

Artichokes à la Provençale 28

* * *

LAMB BRAISED
EN PAPILLOTE 86

—

Mashed Potatoes 122
and seasonal vegetables

* * *

Poached Pears with
Spiced Honey 146

or

Chocolate Cream Shots 154

* * *

Pasta and Pizza

* * *

Nibbles and Appetizers

Mushroom Stock 48
with small vegetables

—

Artichokes à la Provençale 28

—

No-Cook or Low-Cook
Cocktail Hour Platter 12

—

Parmesan, Mushroom and Fennel Salad 36

or

Apple and Fennel Salad 36

—

Green Salad with
Parmesan Vinaigrette 30

—

Martini Olives 14

* * *

Main Dish

Pasta with Tomato Sauce 94

—

Pasta Pepe e Cacio 96

—

Sausage and Spinach Pasta 100

—

Pasta Caponata 98

—

Egg Pizza 104

—

Pissaladière 106

* * *

Dessert

Panna Cotta 132

—

Biscotti vin santo

—

Nougat with seasonal fruit

—

Homemade ice cream with Rice Krispie Brittle 138
or Chocolate Sauce 170

—

Affogato 145

—

Grapes with Port 144

* * *

Asian Meal 1

* * *

Chinese Egg Drop Soup 44

* * *

ASIAN-STYLE PORK LOIN 80

—

Japanese Watercress Salad 35

or

Roasted Vegetables 117–118

* * *

Lychee Frozen Yogurt 136

or

Mango and Frangipane Tarts 163

or

Rice Krispie Brittle 138
and store-bought exotic sorbets

* * *

Asian Meal 2

* * *

Japanese Watercress Salad 35

* * *

A steaming bowlful
HEARTY ASIAN
CHICKEN SOUP 66

* * *

Cardamom Buttons 149
with tea

or

Mandarin Sorbet 138

* * *

For the Holidays 1

* * *

Chicken Liver Mousse with Figs 21

or

Smoked Salmon Mousse 18

or

Oysters 40

* * *

Naturally

TURKEY BREAST WITH
GRAPEFRUIT 74

—

Green vegetables
(baby peas or green beans) and
Braised Beet Salad 34
and Sweet Potato Mash
(omit olives) 123
or Celeriac Mash 123

* * *

Steamed Spiced
Chocolate Pudding 156

or

Assorted sweet platter:
cookies, chocolate, truffles,
fruit, Grapes with Port 144,
nougat

* * *

For the Holidays 2

* * *

Mushroom Stock 48

or

Chicken Liver Mousse 21

* * *

A real treat

DUCK AND TURKEY PIE 76

—

Green salad
Braised Beet Salad 34
Cranberry Sauce 170

* * *

Steamed Spiced
Chocolate Pudding 156

or

Assorted sweet platter:
cookies, chocolate, truffles,
fruit, Grapes with Port 144,
nougat

* * *

For the Holidays 3

* * *

Oysters 40

or

Mushroom Cappuccino 50

* * *

TURKEY CUTLETS PICCATA 72

—

Mashed Potatoes 122
and Roasted Green Beans 118

* * *

It's all good

Chocolate Cream Shots 154

or

Grapes with Port 144

or

Assorted sweet platter:
cookies, chocolate, truffles,
fruit, Grapes with Port 144,
nougat

* * *

Gift Ideas

* * *

Grissini 16

—

Chicken Liver Mousse
with Figs 21

—

Dried Duck Breasts 38

—

Minestrone 42

—

Butternut Squash Soup 47

—

Lemon Oil 176

—

Pepper Oil 176

—

Poached Pears with
Spiced Honey 146

—

Cardamom Buttons 149

—

Truffle Squares 150

—

Almond, Chocolate and
Date Cake 152

—

Chocolate Birthday Cake 158

—

Caramel Spread 166

* * *

* * *

Thank you, thank you, thank you!
I've already told you, but
I'll tell you again and now in writing,
in order or disorder or whatever:
My cooking cannot be measured,
and neither can my thanks;
but they are warmly and uniquely for you.

* * *

Thank you, Stéphan Boucher.
Thanks to you, we did it!

—

A great big thank-you to Daniel Pinard.

—

Thank you to my friends and family
for being a priceless sounding board
while I wrote this book.

—

To the Goodwin Agency,
Marie-Claude Goodwin,
and Patrick Leimgruber,
thank you for being in sync with me.

—

To André Cornellier for believing in this
since forever.

* * *

* * *

Thanks to all
who supported me
throughout the creation of this book:
Louise Pesant,
Michelle Gélinas.

—

A big thank-you to Louise Savoie
and her assistants Jade Martel
and Alain Fournier
for their great availability
and the very beautiful photos.

—

Grazie, Elena, Nino e Antonio.
Steve, thank you.

—

A big thank-you to Pierre Drouin.

—

Thank you to Josée Robitaille
for her wonderful help.

—

Thank you to Colette Brossoit
and Caroline Dumais
for their warm welcome.

—

A big thank-you to Maryse Cantin
for her generosity.

—

Thank you to Mario Mercier,
Marie-Noëlle Turcotte,
Nathalie Bonenfant and everyone on
the great graphics team
at orangetango.

* * *

Thank you to Télé-Québec
for allowing the book
to be named after the show.

—

Thank you to Zone3
for generously participating
in this project.

—

Thank you to Gaz Métro
for their support.

* * *

Thank you to the farmers,
merchants and importers
who care about quality
and the environment and who give
us access to wonderful products.

* * *